A Lean Leader's Guide

Effective emails

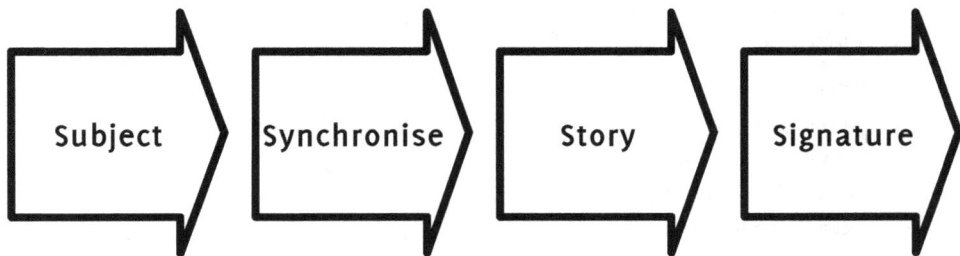

Subject → Synchronise → Story → Signature

Writing and managing great emails

Works by the same author

Lean Presentations — Create outstanding presentations with Lean Six Sigma

- Design principles for presentations, slides and visuals, and handouts.
- How to create business stories using a story arc.
- Designing engagement into presentations.
- How to deal with rogue behaviours.
- Working with questions.
- Avoiding the five presentation wastes.

ISBN	9780993250439
Publisher	Spectaris Ltd.
Published	03 December 2017
Language	English <lang= en-uk>
Pages	160
Binding	perfect-bound Paperback
Interior	Black & white

...so that you can design and deliver an outstanding presentation.

SWOT Analysis — A guide to SWOT Analysis for business studies students. Undertaking a SWOT analysis is a popular strategy tool, and frequently the basis of an assignment for students of business studies. This guide helps you with:

- The critical theory.
- Worked-examples and case-studies.
- Where to look for the factors.
- How to create strategic responses to a situation.
- How to approach a swot assignment.
- Avoiding the usual mistakes.
- References

ISBN	9780993250439
Publisher	Spectaris Ltd.
Published	07 November 2016
Language	English <lang en-uk>
Pages	86
Binding	perfect-bound Paperback
Interior	Black & white

...so you can hand in a great assignment.

Recruitment and selection — Recruitment and selection can be expensive; getting it wrong is even more so. Based on their real-world experiences, Eddie Lunn and Alan Sarsby guide you through the whole project to recruit and select the best person for the role. Includes:

- The benefits of a project oriented approach.
- How to lead and manage the recruitment and selection project.
- How to design assessments, questions, and interviews.

ISBN	9780993250408
Publisher	Spectaris Ltd.
Published	15 April 2015
Language	English <lang en-uk>
Pages	122
Binding	perfect-bound Paperback
Interior	Black & white

How an applicant centred approach brings out the best in candidates and makes the assessment easier for you.

Copyright theft

You should be reading this work as a perfect bound paper book. It is not published in any other form. If you are reading a scanned (and likely, poor quality) pdf, it is not a legitimate copy. Please contact your supplier and require a genuine print.

If you want to share this ebook with a friend, please do so. But it is better all round if you lend it to then for a quick review so your friend can decide to buy their own copy. With their own copy your friend can annotate pages, highlight passages, and generally make it their own.

Thanks.

Notice of Rights

First printing: May 2018

Language <en-gb>

ISBN 978-0-9932504-4-6.

The Leadership Library is an imprint of Spectaris Limited. Registered in England: 05448422

www.leadership-library.co.uk

Copyright

Notice of liability

Trademarks

Third parties

Contents

Email everywhere

Email is now the primary means of communication in organisations. It carries reports, memos, and information exchange among departments and colleagues.

The once 'whilst-you-were-out' notes an assistant stuck on your desk or the bezel of your monitor have been replaced by email. The monthly report that landed in your desk in-tray has been replaced by email. And often, conversations which happened by telephone have been replaced by an exchange of emails. Where once the in-tray was heaped up and overflowing, it is now the email Inbox that overflows.

In this book, the assumption is that you know how to drive your email software application; you know enough of the technical things, for example, how to launch your email application, enter email addresses and add attachments.

But knowing how to drive the software and being a good email citizen are different things.

Driving the software is analogous to passing your driving test. The aim of this work is to help you survive in the busy motorway-like world of corporate email.

1   Lean emails?

The Lean philosophy is made up of a single objective and three supporting principles:

Objective: Value to the customer
The objective in Lean is to deliver value to the customer. The customer is the recipient of your email and they define what is valuable.

Principle: Eliminating waste
In an email, wastes are those parts which distract the reader.

Principle: Respect for humanity
Your recipients are made up of humans, who (hopefully) have the properties of humanity. Respect for humanity probably makes the email a joy to open and read.

Principle: Continuous Improvement
With each use of email there is the opportunity to make it better.

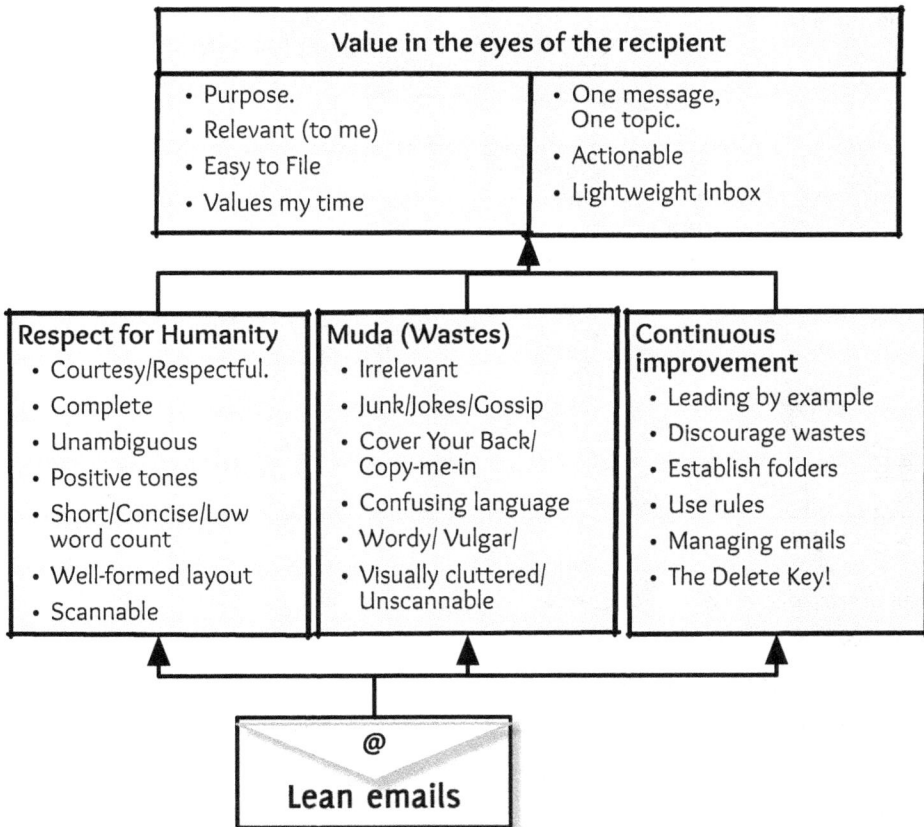

Value in the eyes of the recipient	
• Purpose. • Relevant (to me) • Easy to File • Values my time	• One message, One topic. • Actionable • Lightweight Inbox

Respect for Humanity	Muda (Wastes)	Continuous improvement
• Courtesy/Respectful. • Complete • Unambiguous • Positive tones • Short/Concise/Low word count • Well-formed layout • Scannable	• Irrelevant • Junk/Jokes/Gossip • Cover Your Back/ Copy-me-in • Confusing language • Wordy/ Vulgar/ • Visually cluttered/ Unscannable	• Leading by example • Discourage wastes • Establish folders • Use rules • Managing emails • The Delete Key!

@
Lean emails

2   Email —The ubiquitous medium

Electronic mail was originally a paper-based medium. In the 1980s, a user would logon via a Teletype, then go for a coffee whilst a printer churned out a list of messages. Electronic-mail was electronic-post, it substituted postal mail where correspondents were in different places at different times. As time passed, electronic mail, or e-mail, matured along with the technology supporting it. Email is no longer hyphenated; it is a noun in its own right.

	Sender and receiver are in the same time zone	Sender and receiver are in the different time zone
Sender and receiver are in the *Same* place	*Same time, same place* Face-Face meetings, Talk to each other, Walk over and speak with each other! *Now we ping emails to colleagues sat at the next desk*	*Same place, different time* Sticky notes, memos Job files (job sharing), Messages via an intermediary. *Email is now the means for all these tasks*
Sender and receiver are in *Different* places	*Same time, different place* Telephone, Conference calls and video conferencing, Instant Messaging. Voice over IP *Now we swap emails almost in real-time instead of using the telephone!*	*Different time, different place* Email, Voicemail, Postal mail, Web portals. *Email is now the dominant form of communication*

Email has invaded every aspect of how we communicate with each other. Email is now in every quadrant of the time/place table. With increasing functionality email became the one-size-fits-all approach to messaging. The personal and organisational challenge is not to let email become the only means of communicating. There are some messages that, if delivered by email, can have disastrous consequences, especially where feelings and emotions are involved.

3   The ancient language of emails

3.1   It was highly abbreviated

In the beginning emails had to be brief; it was a restriction imposed by the technology. This restriction led to a culture of writing emails in highly abbreviated forms. A typical email of the time might have been:

> A spk to T abt £ b4 mvg fwd. FAIK not in c/f proj. K.

> Translation — Alan, speak to Ted about budget before moving forward. For all I know, it is not in the cash flow projection. Kevin.

One can see where modern Txt-spk originated! Messages became short, curt, and sometimes (unintentionally) rude. The consequence is that the recipient (whom you might never have met) forms an opinion about you. It might not be what you would like.

3.2   Email etiquette is important

Emails are the dominant form of business communications, they need the same care that you'd give to other forms of correspondence. With emails being quick and casual it is easy to be lazy and easy overlook the need for professionalism.

Three good reasons to be professional with your emails are:

Reputation
Emails carry your personal reputation; they carry the brand of you and your organisation. Writing an email that's a delight to receive elevates your reputation.

Effectiveness
A well-crafted email saves the need for several more. As we'll see later, good quality emails reduce the load on your Inbox.

Liability
Emails are regarded as company correspondence. They have the status of evidence — poor or inappropriately worded emails can land you in trouble.

Remember— with just a few clicks, your confidential message can be shared globally. Think carefully about what you say in an email.

Email is different from other forms of communications. The table following shows a summary of differences, feel free to add your own.

	Written	Telephone	Email
Emotional content	With a longer text, tone can be deduced.	Easy to hear tone/ pitch/inflection of voice.	Tone is guessed – high risk of an incorrect guess!
Humour	With an expertly constructed script, humour can be conveyed to the reader.	Easily achieved with tone of voice, pace, and jocularity.	Difficult, unless the joke is very short, or follows a well-known format. *(eg, 'a crocodile goes into a bar:')*
Tone	Writers use language, to portray the tone of a situation. High wordcount required.	Tone can be heard in the inflexions of speech.	Almost impossible.
Timeliness	Each turn in the conversation is delayed by the transit time of delivery.	Instant. (After the telephone has been answered.)	Can be quick, but speed depends on the recipient being connected, and the transfer speed (bits/s).
Privacy	Depends: A sealed envelope is more private than a postcard.	Private.	Almost none.
Page layout	Designed by the author; the reader sees the same layout.	n/a	What is displayed is unlikely to be the same as the author intended..
Reading	On paper – reading is linear – start to end.	n/a	On-screen – reading is often scanned.
(Add your own)			

4 Creating delightful emails

4.1 The importance of purpose in emails

Without a purpose the email is a waste of time to compose and send. From from the recipient's perspective, it is yet more junk interrupting their personal productivity. Having a purpose helps with both the content and the subject line. The table below shows some examples for business emails. All emails should have a purpose (including those you forward to others).

	To give information	To make a request	To give a response
Purpose	Updates News Sales offers Dispatch notices Announcements.	Request permission Invitations Request information Request help Request authority	Give permission Accept information Give advice Give authorisation Confirm agreement

Creating a purpose.

Use the method of asking yourself, what do I want the receiver:

- to know,

- to think, or

- to do,

    ... as a consequence of receiving your email?

If you can't find a purpose, don't send the email.

Thinking of purpose can be enlightening; for example, what is the *purpose* of forwarding those jokes?

5   Writing a great subject line

5.1   The Subject line is the first impression

According to the old cliché you only get one chance at a first impression. For an email, that first impression is the Subject Line. The subject lines are what we scan down to select an interesting email to open.

Most of us scan throughout our day. We scan headlines in newspapers, menus and faces in a crowd. We scan to choose which articles to read or scan to choose what to eat and who to speak with. Literate humans are very experienced scanners.

It is much the same when scanning down the Inbox. The subject line is the headline and you choose to open, ignore, or delete, based on whether it has grabbed your attention, piqued your interest, or left you cold and bored.

A well-crafted subject line increases the chance of your message being opened rather than deleted. Typically, your reader can see about twelve words (see note below). However we don't scan twelve words, we scan the first few words. Similarly newspaper headlines are typically fewer than ten words to make them easily scannable. A more detailed look at scanning is in §7.2.

Short subject lines make it easy for your recipient to scan. Long subject lines, add hassle for your reader who might need to scroll horizontally to see the whole line.

> Notes
>
> In old teletype email, lines were 80 characters in length. The usual convention was to limit the line length to 72 characters. An average of five characters per word plus a space results in twelve words per line.
>
> The carriage of mechanical typewriters was fitted with a bell that 'tinged' at a pre-set position, usually between the 60th and 72nd character position. The bell reminded the typist to operate the carriage-return bar at the end of the next word and start a new line.

Remember:
A subject line is one line of text. If it is too long, your reader might just give up and delete it instead.

5.2   Elements of a great subject line

The approach to writing good subject lines has many parts:

Write it from recipient's point of view

Make your subject line interesting for your recipient. You might have a purpose in sending an email, but it is not all about you. Giving your reader a reason to be interested means that your email is more likely to be opened. Some key considerations are:

Relevancy — Is the subject matter relevant to the recipient?

Timeliness — Is it timely (or maybe urgent) from the recipient's point of view?

Importance — Is it significant to the recipient?

Write subject lines as headlines

Subject lines are initially seen out of context (often in a separate list). Write the subject line as a self-contained and scannable micro-message. Aim for about eight words as a maximum.

> Note — A newspaper headline is in close proximity to its associated story. This is not usually true for email subject lines; they are often presented as a list without context. The subject line has to stand on its own merit.

Value in the first words

Write the first few words to convey something of value to your recipient. Remember the recipient is scanning a long list of subject lines and they tend to look down the left-hand side of the list at the first one or two words only. Critical information belongs at the beginning of the subject line, not the end. Subject lines are more attractive when you include actions, imperatives, or benefit phrases. If you can, start the subject line with a verb or the key noun. A subject line made up of a string of nouns is unlikely to grab anyone's attention.

Concise

Omit the articles *a, an, the,* and so on. Precise grammar in a full sentence is not needed in a subject line.

Business words

Use everyday business terms to make it obvious what the message is about. Obviously subject-matter specific words are required if your recipient has the same understanding. Otherwise plain English is the preferred route. And clever puns or cute phrases don't work so well in business emails.

5 Ws and 1 H

The classic way of creating interest in any form of communication is the 5Ws and 1H checklist. The approach was made famous in Rudyard Kipling's poem—Six Serving Men[1]. These five W's and one H should be viewed from the recipient's perspective.

What — is this email about?

Why — is the email relevant to the recipient?

When — is something going to happen/has happened?

How — is the recipient going to do something?

Where — is the recipient to go for the action?

Who — is involved? Includes the recipient and others.

It is almost impossible to include all these in a subject line, and to do so would overwhelm it. However, if you are able to include at least two, your subject line becomes more engaging. Compare the two emails in the screenshot below.

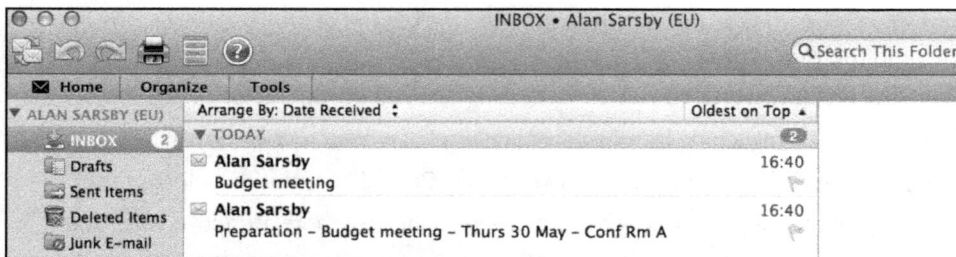

The first email has an uninspiring subject line. It fails the *so what* test, if you're not involved in budgeting — *so what.* If you're in the accounting department, you might receive hundreds of similar messages *so what — which budget meeting?*

---

1   http://en.wikipedia.org/wiki/Six_Honest_Serving_Men

The second email's subject line has:

Action Preparation — a reminder.
What   Budget meeting.
When   Thursday 20 May.
Where   Conference room A.

Examples

Uninspiring subject line	Attention grabbing subject line
Meeting	Cancelled - Friday (date). Team budget meeting.
Agenda	Team away-day — 1 March — Agenda
Invoice	Please authorise - Invoice AB123 (attached)
Enquiry	Help needed — do you have 3 widgets I can borrow?
Update	Update: Simplified procedure for buying small items
Training guide	2016 Training Brochure — Ready for distribution
Big news!	New marketing campaign for November
Payment confirmation	Payment confirmation — Order P41414
Printing contact	Contact for printing the November catalogue
Product	Recommend product launch 5 November
Opportunity	Invitation - Would you present at our conference?
Information	May I borrow the specification for oil-free chains?
<no subject>	Nothing to look at here!

A new trend is to append a tag to the end of a subject line to give an extra indication of what's inside. Using some of the examples from above, they might appear like this:

- Team away-day, 1 March - Agenda [pdf]

- 2018 Services Brochure — Ready for distribution [video link]

- Simplified procedure for buying small items [link]

As always, remember your recipient. If these tags help your recipient, use the tag, if they confuse, don't.

5.3   A few things to avoid in subject lines

Recall that the subject line is the first impression and, hopefully, you'd like to give a good first impression. To finish this section on subject lines there are a few things to avoid. Some of these could cause your recipient to press delete instantly, some are turn-offs and others might end up as junk or spam.

Avoid personalisation

It might be tempting to include the recipient's name in the subject line. For example: *Alan - send me your CV.* Consider how your recipient reacts to this? It can be interpreted as being over-familiar especially with unsolicited contact; then deleted.

In this example, a stranger is giving me a command
Make sure you write this down Alan - Exclusive Notebook Deals.

Avoid SHOUTING

Typing in all-capitals is the equivalent of shouting. We mention this again later, but the notion of shouting in a subject line is a turn-off. The one small exception, to be used sparingly, is a single word at the beginning of the subject line for extremely important, time-sensitive, messages. For example: CANCELLED-this afternoon's product review. Even this is risky. With a message like this, a phone around might be more reliable.

Avoid blank subject lines

Blank subject lines <no subject> create hassle for your reader. Without the subject line, the recipient must look elsewhere to decide whether to open it. The 'From' field might help to identify the sender is, and from that, make a guess at its importance. But otherwise, emails with a blank subject line deserve to be moved directly to the deleted items folder.

Don't write half a sentence

...that is finished in the main body of the message. It is disorienting for the reader to backtrack from the opening words of the message to re-read the subject line. Remember, the Subject line is often separated from the message.

Is your subject line triggering the junk filter

There are many reasons that emails end up in the junk mail folder: one is the choice of words you use in the subject line. Certain words trigger the spam filter: among these are, *Sale, Free, Call now, Order, Medicines,* etc.

Certain words, or words in close proximity to other words, identify the email as suspicious to a spam filter. The importance of using straightforward business words in the subject line should not be underestimated. The table following shows a selection of real email titles automatically moved to the junk mail folder.

Subject lines that end up in the junk mail folder	Reason
Free stripper	The email was from a builder's supply company and the stripper was a wallpaper remover. But 'free' and 'stripper' was more than the spam filter could cope with!
Are you free on June 8th Edinburgh Airport?	Spam filter triggered by 'Free' in the first few words
Account Alert !	Excessive exclamations
Hello <ADDRESS style="DISPLAY: none"></ADDRESS> <CITE style="DISPLAY: none"></CITE><EM style="DISPLAY: none"></EM>	This is bulk-generated spam, but a careless programmer included the scripting variables in the subject line.
Re: Brand name luxury watches	A supplier of fake products.

There are many more reasons for an email being moved into the junk folder; these include known source addresses, heuristics to detect certain patterns, and a catalogue of known scams.

It is worth checking the spam or junk folder occasionally to be sure that innocent messages haven't been captured.

5.4   Summary — The benefit of a great subject line

We're all busy people, and your recipient benefits from your professionalism in separating the important emails from the dross.

(And as a by-product—it contributes to your personal reputation.)

- The subject line stands alone—it is a micro message from you to your reader.

- A good subject line helps your recipient to action the message. For example, where to file it.

- Subject Lines are often displayed as a list, separate from the email text.

Checklist:

1 — Check your Inbox and pick out the attention-grabbing subject lines. Use these as ideas for your own subject lines.

2 — Check the sent items folder and pick out the attention-grabbing subject lines you have sent to other people.

3 — Check your junk mail folder and work out why things have been moved there. Then use this knowledge to help with really great subject lines.

One final note ...

Do you succumb to the lazy method of finding an old email as a quick way to send a message to someone by opening it and pressing 'Reply'?

What often happens, is that one forgets to change the subject line and the new message is not relevant to the old subject line. Remember to change the subject line when replying; otherwise you're making it hard for your recipient.

6   The postcard principle — Part 1

6.1   How big is an e-postcard?

Email software often offers users a choice of layouts. As a user, you can select, typically, which panes you see. The picture below shows a common layout.

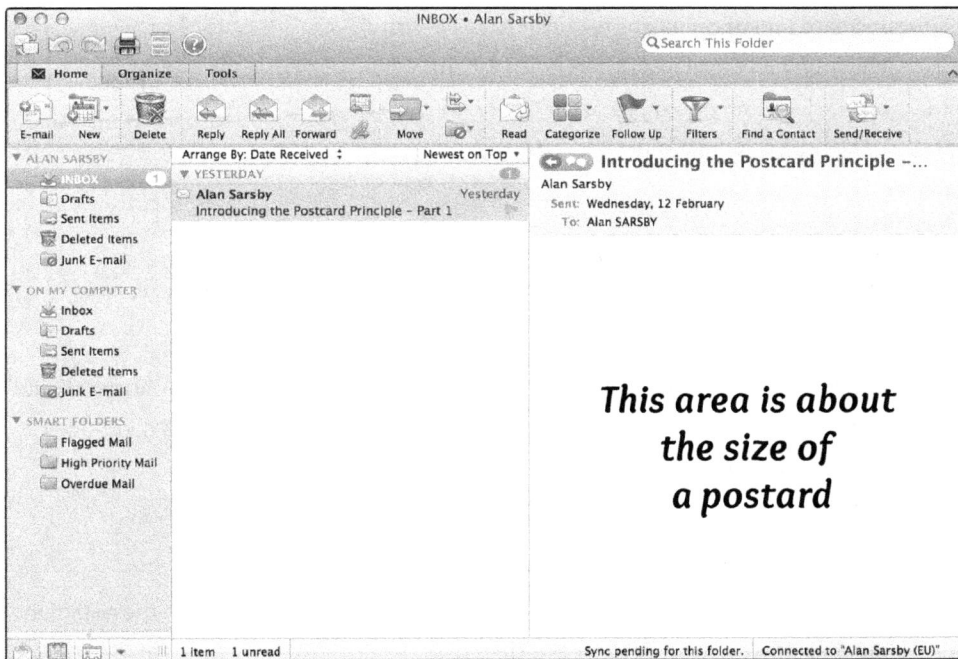

On a laptop, a common screen size for business users is approximately 15" across the diagonal. This is slightly larger than a piece of A4 paper.

Desk exercise:

Take a sheet of A4 paper and cut out the area of the message pane. Remember to cut off the area for headers, the status area, and scroll bars. Cut off any area you cannot type into.

How much is left for the real message?

After you've completed the exercise, you'll probably be holding a piece of paper about the same size as a postcard. You've discovered the postcard principle. The real amount of space for an email message is about the same as that on a postcard. *So What?* The answer is that long emails are more difficult for your recipient to process. In keeping with our theme of sending emails that are a delight to receive, a successful email is short and concise.

6.2   Principles for concise emails

> "I'm sorry for writing such a long letter, I did not have time to write a short one."
>
> Attributed variously to Blaise Pascale, Abraham Lincoln, Winston Churchill, Mark Twain, Cicero, and others

Our e-postcard limitation means we need to approach writing an email in a different way from other forms of written communication. There are three principles for writing short and effective emails.

One email covers one topic

By writing emails that cover only one topic at once you make it easy for your recipient to manage the message.

For example, if you send an email containing five topics. Two are trivial and would normally be deleted, and three are important, but different, topics. Where does your recipient file it?

Help your recipient by making it easy for them to process your message.

Make your point — then stop writing. Stop!

Remember that emails should have a purpose. Reach that purpose in the minimum number of words and sentences—then stop.

The apparent empty space in the postcard might tempt you to add more, for example, social chatter *(did you see last night's football—what a goal, eh)*. Don't. Stick to the point; make the point, then stop writing.

Write concisely

There is an art to writing concisely—this is so important for emails, that a whole section of this guide is devoted to it.

Remember

The goal is to create emails that are a delight to receive. And your bonus is a reputation for being a great communicator.

7 Structure of an email

7.1 Synchronise with your reader

The best communications have been thought out and have an underlying structure. It is tempting to think that email is so casual that no planning and structure is needed. Sorry, but this is not so.

The essential structure of an email is to synchronise with your reader, then once synchronised, continue telling your message. We all know how it feels to listen to a message when the speaker starts in the middle of the story. But with an email there's no way to wave our arms in the air and ask the speaker to start again from the beginning! Remember too, that your message is likely to be one of hundreds that the recipient is working their way through—make it easy for them.

The first line in the body of an email performs the job of synchronisation. Once read, the reader should know the context of what follows. This synchronisation phase is useful in all forms of communication, but vital in an email.

In business, email is a fast and furious medium; your recipient could be subconsciously thinking about the previous email even though they are reading yours. Hence the first few lines in the body of the email should establish a synchronised context between you and your recipient.

Some examples:

Yes, proceed as you suggest	This is almost meaningless, or at best it forces the reader to scroll down to the original message to discover what was suggested.
You asked about the approach to the awards ceremony – please proceed as you suggested.	This reminds the recipient of the context and the question (possibly asked several days earlier).

It is helpful to, start with a synchronising statement.

> *Thanks for letting me know about the Trustees visit. ...*

> *The project Saturn board meeting is next Thursday, 25 July.*

Tip — if the project has a name, use it to help synchronise your recipient, who might be involved in many projects.

After synchronising — then tell the message.

The postcard principle encourages brief direct delivery of the message, and this affects how your message is crafted.

7.2   Layout for scanning

We've mentioned previously that people tend to scan when reading from a screen. So our aim is to create an email that is a delight to receive, and to compose it so the recipient can scan it. There are two main ways of achieving this — using bullet points, and using sub-headings.

Bullet points
Bullet points have similar characteristics to subject lines. Short succinct points with the key words near the beginning of the line. Bullet points tend to be a few words or, at most, a few lines.

Sub-headings
Sub headings — are like bullet points and crafted in the same manner, but instead of indicating just a few lines, they indicate a distinct topic or subsection. The 5Ws and 1H technique helps you to write scannable headings.

Layout for scanning makes it easier for your recipient to find the item they are looking for. For example if, on the morning of the meeting, the recipient only wants to know where to go, a simple scan down the message delivers the critical information.

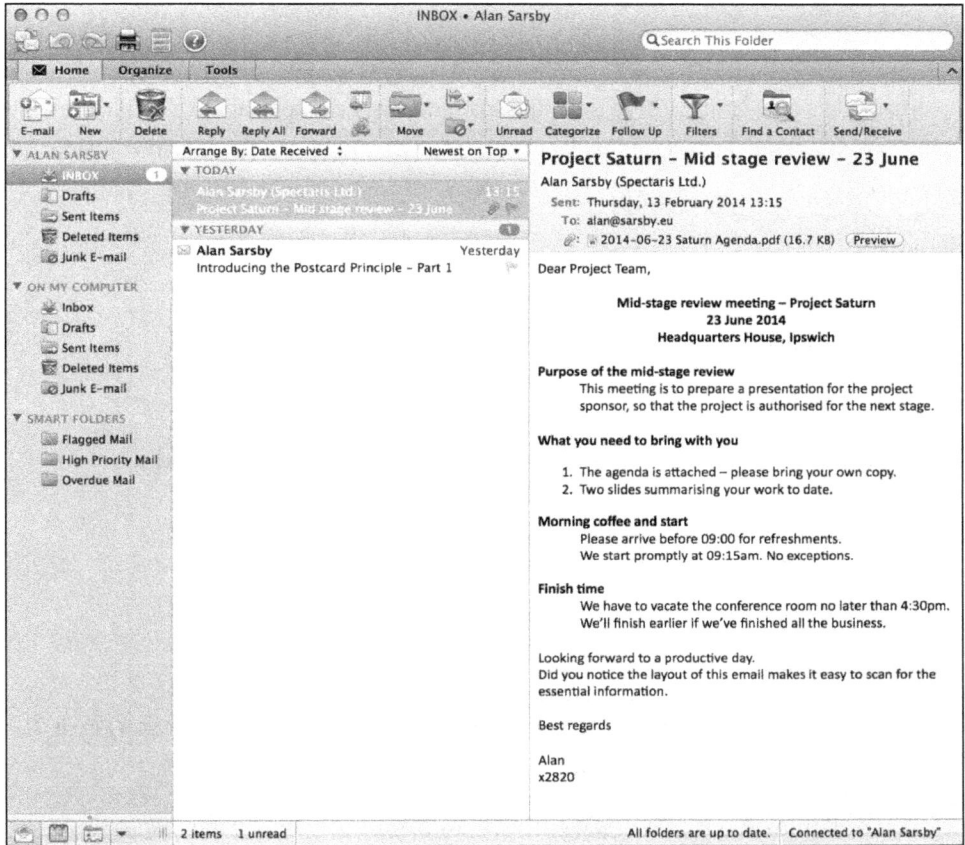

The layout makes it easy to scan, and it can print on one side of paper for easy reference.

The example above illustrates an email inviting people to a meeting. Each sub-heading indicates what type of content follows. This email follows the postcard principle and the layout for scanning.

- The email has a clear subject line, with an identifying project name, a 'Why' (a mid stage review) and a date (the 'When').

- A summary title in the main body of the text. The tone is professional.

- A Purpose — *persuade the sponsor to continue with the project.*

- A direction of what to bring with you — *two clear actions.*

- The start and finish times. *(With a motivation to finish early!)*

7.3   The postcard summary

An email is like a postcard. There is limited space to carry our message, if you write emails with a huge word-count, you are making it hard for your recipient to read and understand your message.

Summary:

To create emails that are a delight to receive then remember:

- One topic per message.

- Keep it short.

- Synchronise your recipient so they know what they are about to read.

- Put the message in a structure, so that it can be scanned, and

- Easily acted upon.

Personal review

1 — Examine some of your recent emails (often in your sent items folder) review those that were more like novels. How could they be made scannable?

2 — Review some multi-topic emails. How many could be separated into single-topic messages. Remember this makes it easier for your recipient to file the message in the right place.

8 The toolkit for clarity

8.1 The benefits of clarity

What happens when your recipient doesn't understand your email?

Usually one of two things:

> **Delete** — Your message is deleted, in which case you've failed as an effective communicator.

> **Wastes** — Your recipient wastes their time trying to decode your intention, gives up and sends you a message back asking for clarification. You then waste your time clarifying what you originally meant and reply with another email. In total, three emails have been exchanged and two people have wasted valuable time. Imagine how this scales up if you sent the original email to a team of five people.

8.2 Write your email from the recipient's perspective

For emails, apply the KISS principle (see note below) and at the same time being clear and unambiguous. Remember the postcard principle: you have limited space. Remember too, that your recipient might have a limited attention span.

Our goals for writing clear messages are:

- To remove the distractions.

- Make it easy for you recipient to process. (One email contains one topic.)

- To keep the message short and clear.

> Note — KISS— an acronym with several (similar) meanings, for example,
> Keep it Short and Sweet, or Keep it Simple, Stupid!

8.3   Remove the distractions

A distraction is anything that interferes with the understanding of the message. Two big distractions are:

Off-topic content is a distraction.
Wandering off topic, adding unnecessary content, office gossip. Remember the one email/one topic rule.

Spelling and grammar.
Spolling mistooks and poor gramer distract the reader from your message. See what I mean? Spelling and grammar are so important we should say a bit more about these topics:

8.4   Spelling is important

Poor spelling shouts out at your recipient and, instead of reading the content of your important email, they only see your unprofessional approach.

A modern email application often puts squiggly lines under words that are not in its dictionary. There really is no excuse for sending an email with a spelling mistake. Be aware that not all email systems do the spell check automatically; for some systems it has to be initiated manually. If you forget, then off goes your email and off goes your reputation.

By the way, computer spell checking can be fooled. The English language has little quirks waiting to thwart spelling checkers, for example:

Homophones — Words that sound alike but have different meanings:

> new and knew

> to, too, and two

Homographs — Words that have the same spelling but are different in meaning and pronunciation, for example:

> lead (noun) the metal,

> lead (noun) as in a dog lead,

> or to lead (verb) as in to lead a team.

Just for fun work through the poem below. You'll see the words are spelt correctly but many are the wrong words.

I halve a spelling chequer,
It came with my pea see.
It plainly marks four my revue
Mistakes I dew knot sea.

Eye strike a key and type a word
And weight four it two say
Weather eye am wrong oar write
It shows me strait aweigh.

As soon as a mist ache is maid
It nose bee fore two long
And eye can put the era rite
Its rarely ever wrong.

I've scent this massage threw it,
And I'm shore your pleased too no
Its letter prefect in every weigh;
My checker tolled me sew.

A search on the Internet shows many variations of this poem for example see: www.greaterthings.com/Humor/Spelling_Chequer.htm

To overcome this spell-checking problem, the usual advice applies:

- Read your message out aloud, speaking every word as written — not what's inside your head.

- Save your email as a draft and come back to it a few hours or a day later. You'll be more likely to see the errors after a rest.

- For important messages, perhaps where your reputation is at risk, ask a friend to read your important email — before you send it!

8.5   Grammar can be abbreviated, but not ignored.

As we saw earlier, emails can be short and curt, but getting the basics wrong makes you look unprofessional and there goes your reputation.

Verbs and nouns

Grammar doesn't come more basic than verbs and nouns. For example:

> Affect is a verb, as in *to affect*.
>
> Effect is a noun, as in *the effect*.

Apostrophes

An apostrophe indicates possession. For example:

> John's ball
>
> its' doesn't exist, it should be its or it's

Elisions — missing letters

An elision indicates omission of letters where two words are contracted, it's (it is) an important indicator of casual rather than formal writing. The elision and apostrophe, both use a single quotation (') character. For example:

> it's — it is, or it has
>
> you've — you have
>
> you're — you are

Tense

Using the wrong tense can easily change the meaning of your email.

> Fred looked at the web page I had been working on.
> — Suggests that I worked on the web page sometime in the past.
>
> Fred looked at the web page I have been working on.
> — Suggests that I am still working on the web page.

Pronouns

A pronoun is a substitute for a real noun. The three basic categories of pronoun are first person indicating the speaker, the second person indicating the person being spoken to, and the third person indicating someone else. Pronouns save space, but take care with the clarity of who is accountable for an action. For example :

First person — *I completed the project on Tuesday.*
It is clear that I am the sender of the email. However, if you use the first person plural *we* (We completed the assignment...) you might be disguising who the other person is.

Second person — *Thanks for your review the project Tuesday.*
Usually it is clear who the second person is — it is the person reading the email. However, if you sent your message to multiple recipients then it is not clear to whom 'you' or 'your' refers. If you need to give an action to someone, refer to them by name and not a pronoun.

Third person — *They completed the project on Tuesday.*
Using the third person is a frequent cause of ambiguity. Because 'they' refers to someone who is neither the writer nor the recipient, it leaves open who 'they' are.

Punctuation

The brevity of emails reduces the scope for punctuation errors. Brevity can help, you still need to take care. Mistakes in punctuation can change the meaning and create ambiguity.

For example:

Save water and waste paper could be a message to use less water and consequently use fewer paper towels. Equally it could be a message to recycle leftover used water and recycle used paper towels. Your recipient makes the choice, not you.

Just for fun, compare the two Dear John letters that follow. Both versions have identical words, but different punctuation.

One is a love letter, the other a good-riddance letter.

Dear John,

I want a man who knows what love is all about. You are generous, kind, thoughtful. People who are not like you admit to being useless and inferior. You have ruined me for other men. I yearn for you. I have no feelings whatsoever when we're apart. I can be forever happy - will you let me be yours?

Mary

Dear John,

I want a man who knows what love is. All about you are generous, kind, thoughtful people, who are not like you. Admit to being useless and inferior. You have ruined me. For other men, I yearn. For you, I have no feelings whatsoever. When we're apart, I can be forever happy. Will you let me be?

Yours, Mary

Note — The Dear John example is a grammarian's joke. It appears in several books and an Internet search returns thousands of results. At the time of writing, the original source has not been discovered.

Grammatical errors often the consequence of repeated editing. The message started out in one direction, then afterthoughts changed a part of a sentence and the whole paragraph became a grammatical tangle.

By now, you can a guess the suggested solution :

Read your message out aloud, speaking every word as written. Do not read words that are not there. For elisions, read out the words without the omission — for example, when you see *it's,* speak aloud *it is.* If the message still makes sense, you've *(you have)* probably got it right.

For important emails, ask a friend to read your email — before you send it!

8.6   Reduce the word-count and increase the clarity

This is back to our Postcard Principle. The aim is to say what we need to say in the fewest number of words. Clarity comes from careful use of language and construction of the message.

Of the many culprits of excess words and ambiguity, a few of these are:

Abstract phrases — invites assumptions

Use concrete expressions whenever you can. If you say something like "see you tomorrow" what does it mean to your recipient who opens the email the following morning? A concrete phrase is "See you on Thursday morning at 10am" (in this case the clarity is worth the extra few words.)

Auxiliary verbs — need extra words

Auxiliary verbs need a main verb to work with, this increases the word count. Some examples:

> *...will contain*, could be simplified to *contains*

> *The volume will be increased* could be simplified to *The volume is increased*, or even simpler to: *increases the volume.*

Circumlocutions — say it in a round about way

> Instead of *at a later time*, simply say *later*.

Double negatives — create confusion

Double negatives increase the word-count and reduce clarity. The interpretation of a double negative depends on the reader's version of English: two negatives can cancel each other to leave a positive; alternatively, it is a reinforcement of the negative. Your reader makes the choice, not you!

> *It's not unusual* — a subtle way of saying it is common.

> *I don't know nothing* — Estuary English[2] for I don't know anything

---

2   Estuary English is a dialect and accent associated with the East of London and the Thames estuary.

Internet speak — saves space but obscures meaning

IMNSHO this is NAGI. HTH.

> Translation — In my not so humble opinion this is not a good idea. Hope this helps. Is your recipient fluent in net-speak?

Jargon saves space — but adds exclusivity

Jargon saves space, only use jargon if you're certain that the recipient shares the same *meaning* of it. Take a moment to decide if Plain English would be better.

Long words — use up more space

Most long words have a shorter equivalent.
Use the shorter word.

Negative phrases — adds words and loses clarity

A negative phrase conveys what you want to restrict but leaves open what you'd like to achieve. Positive phrasing often requires fewer words.

For example

Negative phrase	Positive phrase
Does not include	Leaves out
Not often	Rarely
Don't forget to:	Remember to:

Passive voice — increases words and reduces responsibility

Using the active voice for your message has a huge impact on clarity of your message. The active voice usually needs fewer words than the passive voice, and it adds clarity by associating the doer with the action.

For example:

Passive voice	Active voice
The ball was thrown by John	John threw the ball
A frog was kissed	The princess kissed the frog
The application must be completed by the student and received by the bursar's office by 1 June. [17 words]	The bursar must receive your application by 1 June. [9 words]

Political correctness — obscures the meaning

Political correctness needs more words and frequently uses coded euphemisms, which need de-coding by the recipient.

Straightforward English is easier for your recipient to understand and less likely to be misinterpreted.

Long sentences — take longer to read

In an email short sentences are good. A dissertation is a good place for erudite vocabulary and complex structures to show off your knowledge and increase the word count — but not in an email.

Tautologies — say it twice

The repetition of meaning using different words. Just say things once! For example: added bonus — a bonus is an added extra (for example, extra pay) so expanding 'added bonus' results in 'added added extra'.

8.7   A note about dates

If you include a date in your message, type the month as a word. For example, say 5 June 2018 rather than 5/6/18.
Some correspondents interpret the all-number format as May 6, 2011.

A dental receptionist told they often have a spate of missed appointments by patients who misread the abbreviated date formats and turn up a month early, or a day late (5/6/2018). After some negotiations (their IT developer didn't understand the problem), appointments are now printed in full — 5 June 2018.

The international standard notation for a date is ISO 8601. The recommended notation for dates is:

Year as four digits, represented as yyyy

The month as two digits, represented as mm

The date as two digits, represented as dd.

Each component may be separated by characters to aid reading. These separators can be: A hyphen (-), or a solidus (/) commonly referred to as a 'slash'.
The most commonly used is the hyphen.

Some examples:

5 June 2011, is 2011-06-05.
It is clear, unambiguous, and common in the technological world.

5/5/2018 could mean: 5 May 2018, or May 5, 2018 (a alias case where the meaning is the same!). In international format it is unambiguous 2018-05-05 (yyyy-mm-dd).

12/13/2018 doesn't make sense — there is no such thing as the 12th day of the thirteenth month. Your reader has to back-track and read it again in the opposite direction to *assume* it means 13 December 2018. In ISO format it is an unambiguous 2018-12-13.

11-11-11
There is an option in international date formats to abbreviate the century to two digits. However this changes the visual shape of the information. To UK readers, it looks like a bank's sort code so your recipient has to double check.
(This one is 11 November 2011.)

8.8   Some tones don't work in emails

Whilst email is quick, easy and informal, there are a few things that don't work, especially in a business context.

8.8.1. Sarcasm

For some people sarcasm is their normal mode of communicating. They find fault with everything and are generally negative. In real encounters it is easier to manage these people because we can see their expressions and others around us can provide a balancing view, but not in emails. The absence of visual and vocal clues makes it easy for even slight amounts of negativity to come across as sarcasm.

The early days of email recognised this problem, and a culture of smiley faces made up from ordinary text characters developed. These are known as emoticons, (a contraction of emotional icons)

A straightforward smiley face is	:-)
or for a big smile or grin	:-))
for lightweight sarcasm, a raised eyebrow	;-)
for stronger sarcasm it is the devilish grin	:->

If you've not come across these emoticons, turn your head to the left and look at the motifs again — you'll see the faces. The trouble is that not everyone understands these little codes, so once again you're making it hard for your reader to work out what's going on or, to put it the other way around, even easier to misunderstand your intention. These little emoticons don't excuse sarcasm. Fortunately, there is a simple cure:

- Express everything in a positive tone,

- Read your message out aloud, and

- For important emails, ask a colleague to read it.
  Your colleague has more chance of detecting unintentional sarcasm that you cannot see nor hear.

8.8.2. Metaphors

We use metaphors in everyday language. For example: *as useless as a chocolate teapot*. Clearly, a chocolate teapot would melt when boiling water is poured in. Except that even this simple metaphor doesn't work where the culture is to drink iced tea, even a chocolate teapot might have a use! There are thousands of these metaphors — they add variety and colour to casual messages. In a professional context they don't always help with the clarity of your message and invite assumptions, which in turn invite more emails to clutter up your Inbox.

8.8.3. Business clichés

Business clichés, also known as 'consultant-speak' and 'management-speak' litter our communications. For example, thinking outside the box, paradigm shift, and take it to the next level. These phrases sound convincing but are ambiguous and difficult to quantify. There are more of these jargonistic phrases in Appendix 3.

8.9   Summary

Email is a written form of communication. It needs the same care you'd give to other written work.

- Look at your message from the recipient's point of view.

- Remove distractions.

- Check your spelling and grammar — they are important.

- Take care with your tone of voice.

- The email postcard has very limited space — use it wisely and effectively.

9 WYSIWYG – not in emails

9.1 The recipient's perspective

The notion of What You See Is What You Get (WYSIWYG) has been around since the 1980s. We're used to typing into our word processors or graphics applications and seeing exactly the same thing on the printed output. This is not true for emails and it is a false assumption that what you type is how the recipient sees it. Your recipient controls how an email is viewed, not you.

Some reasons for this include:

- Different sized areas for the Postcard pane.
  Re-sizing the pane causes text to re-flow to fit within the new shape.

- Different fonts in the computer.
  Even the same font has different versions and displays text differently. (See the next section on fonts.)

- Different capabilities.
  It is common to send emails using the same underlying code used in web pages. However, email applications don't support all the codes and styles of a web browser. What is displayed to your recipient is likely to be different from what is displayed on your own screen.

- Graphics can be blocked. There are very good reasons for this.

- Only plain text might be displayed.
  Some users prefer to see plain text rather than graphically rich text layouts. Your recipient controls this choice, not you.

This list could go on and on, but hopefully you get the idea.

Assume that what you see, and what your recipient sees are different.

9.2   A note about fonts

If you've a modern computer, it probably has about a hundred fonts pre installed. Some applications install extra fonts and your corporate IT services might have added a few more. it is also possible that you have a corporate font licensed separately. The result is a good deal of creative choice. It is unlikely that your recipient has the same fonts as you — even in the same organisation where the IT folks have standard builds and configurations.

Even the same font is likely to be a different version. The differences among versions include kerning (the space between character pairs), leading, (the space between lines), character sets (for example, ã ä ạ̈ æ ǽ å — just a few of the letter 'a' variations).

The example below shows the result of applying a calligraphic font (very tempting to do in a signature line) and the resulting font substitution by the recipient's computer.

What you see	What your recipient sees
Alan	Alan
Formatted with the calligraphic typeface Zapfino	The recipient does not have Zapfino on their computer, so a font substitution takes place

The few compatible fonts

Arial	Times New Roman
Comic Sans	Tahoma
Georgia	Trebuchet
Lucida Grande	Verdana

Even this list is optimistic — it only covers Microsoft Windows and Apple Macintosh operating systems. It means that your creativity is a little stunted when it comes to emails.

9.3　Summary

Fonts in emails are a good example of where less is more. The fewer and more common the font, the more likely the message appears as you intended when your recipient reads it. Using a common font is a more reliable way to get your message across.

Notes

Just so you know — Comic Sans is a love it or hate it typeface, and many designers refuse to have it on their systems. For fun go to www.comicsanscriminal.com/

By the way — the Comic Sans typeface seems popular in big organisations as a way of softening their bureaucratic image. It doesn't work, but that's another story.

9.4　Background colours

A modern email application gives us many creative options to make our messages look pretty, by colouring the background, or placing a background picture. Sometimes this is helpful, and often not.

9.5　Be considerate with in-line graphics

Adding pictures to emails is simple and effective (assuming it fits with your purpose). Pictures can be added as an attachment, or added in-line with the text, often by drag-and-drop from a folder. There is a problem with adding an in-line graphic — it might be too big. Big in this case refers to the pixel dimensions of the image.

A typical computer monitor is typically 2000 pixels wide. The working space using the postcard principle reduces this to about 600 — 1000 pixels. If you drag in the image from earlier in this section, it is 3888 pixels wide and this is too big for the postcard. Your email application might be clever enough to scale the image so it fits inside your sending pane; however, the real problem is what happens when the recipient opens it. It is sometimes the case that the email application displays the pixels as they are, without scaling the image and your recipient only sees the top-left of the image. And unless your recipient is technically competent, it is more difficult to save this image from the message to their computer.

Be considerate when attaching image files. Either:

- Add the image as an attachment.

- If you have to put images in-line with the text, reduce the file size in a photo editor so that it fits within the width of your email postcard.

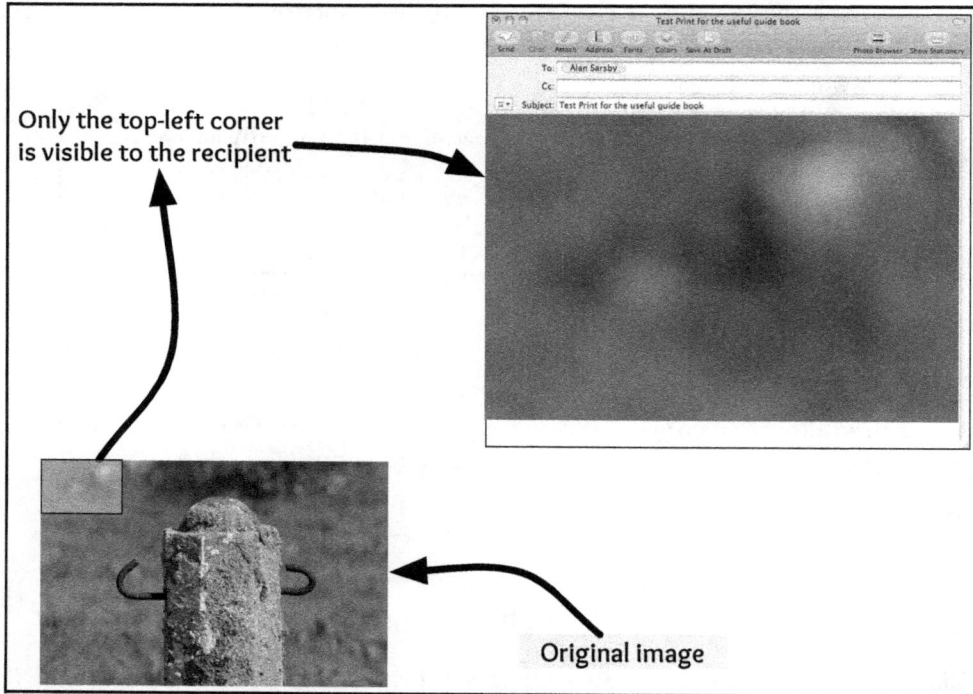

Only the top-left corner is visible to the recipient

Original image

Note: It is worth remembering that some email services automatically move in-line graphics out of the main body of the email, and append them as a attachment. You don't get the choice; the email application or server does this.

9.6   Spaces and tabs

Using the spacebar to make text align with the line above doesn't work. The font and the internal information in the font about how to space pairs of characters define the width of a space. The recipient's font is likely to be different to yours, so to make alignment work, use the tab key instead.

9.7   Summary

Email is a What You See Is **Not** What You Get (WYSI-N-WYG) medium. Your recipient has substantial control over how email messages are displayed on their screens.

- Your recipients control whether they see your graphics. They can force their system into displaying plain text only.

- You and your recipients are unlikely to have the same fonts on your systems. Even fonts with the same name (for example, Verdana) have different versions and hence display slightly differently.

- Unusual fonts are substituted by the recipients' systems and display differently.

- Use the common fonts only. Fancy fonts don't work are victim to substitution.

- Never copy your corporate font to someone else — without a licence to do this it is illegal — you and your organisation could be at risk.

- Leave the background plain.

For WISIWYG — less is more. Think KISS.

10 Sending

10.1 The Courtesy challenge

Some emails need to be sent to more than one person. Examples Include newsletters, team updates, and so on. There are three ways to send one email to many recipients:

	When to use	When not to use
To:	This is the normal use. To direct the email to a specific group of people, who know each other, say a project team.	When there are a large number of recipients, say, everyone in the organisation. Instead, use a mail group or a BCC list.
CC:	Additional recipients who need to know the message contents. It is possible in some email systems to exclude the attachments from those in the cc list. Use also to inform people when they are mentioned in the email but not part of the action.	To cover your back by copying (usually senior) people into an email conversation to prevent yourself being blamed for something. You can annoy a lot of people this way. And you'll gain an unwelcome reputation.
BCC:	Large number of recipients. Use when the email addresses should be kept confidential.	To secretly copy someone in on the email. (When you are found-out, your reputation becomes damaged.)

Note: The abbreviation CC is from the era of the mechanical typewriter. It meant Carbon Copy. A typist would load the roller with extra sheets of paper interleaved with carbon-impregnated paper. When the letter hammer struck the ribbon, the shape of the letter would be imprinted on the outer sheet of paper this was the master or top-copy. The force of the letter hammer is strong enough to transfer the carbon from the impregnated paper through to the paper behind. This would become the carbon copy and was sent to specific people, usually named in the letter. Other carbon copies were known as flimsies, these were created the same way as a normal carbon copy, but on thin (inexpensive) paper. In email, CC usually means Courtesy Copy. The modern abbreviation, BCC, is Blind Courtesy Copy. The receiver sees only their own address and does not see other peoples' email addresses. This is helpful to comply with data protection and privacy policies — it prevents email addresses being shared.

10.2   Sending your email to the right person

It might be obvious but you should send your email to the correct person!

For corporate email, it is likely that you'll use something like a Global Address List or a directory to search, pick, and insert addressees. Be careful. Large organisations often have many John Smiths, Bill Sykes, and Tom Johnsons. One might be a director, the other a maintenance technician.

Beware of pre-defined group lists, for example, 'All networked staff'. One needs to be aware that everyone in the 'All networked staff' group might be in different geographical places, in widely different job functions. So an email concerning roadworks behind the London office is of no relevance to the staff in the Manchester office.

As always, keep in mind the relevance to your recipient. In the example below, the sender has used a scattergun approach and sent the message to four groups in the research institution. It is reasonable to assume that some individuals are in more than one group, so they are going to receive multiple copies of the message.

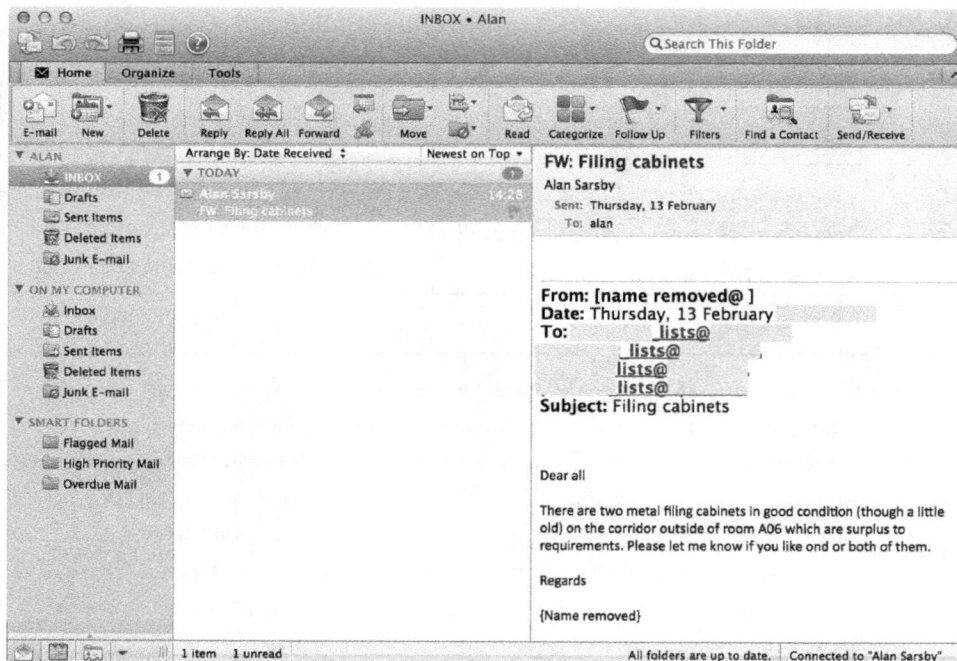

Note — this email has been edited to protect the guilty! By the way, the subject line is uninformative — you might just delete this one!

10.3   Two features to annoy your recipient

10.3.1. Priority

If you set every message to high-priority, what does it say about you? It could be interpreted as 'self important.'

Historically, priority had a network meaning. It flagged the message with a delivery target (a time). Some clever email switches were able to process the message more quickly — a kind of queue jumping — but it came at a price. If the message couldn't be delivered on time, a failure notification was sent back to the originator and the email was discarded. Setting the priority to high often made the quality of service worse!

> Note
>
> The term email switch is shorthand for the technical term Message Transfer Agent. Message transfer agents are the intermediate systems that move your email from your sending system to the destination system. An email might traverse several message transfer agents to reach the destination.

Nowadays, when the priority is set to something other than normal, your recipient sees an indicator showing the priority, for example, high-priority. And even this assumes that the receiver has turned on the column that displays the icon for urgent. Within the message, a visual indicator shows the urgent status — and this becomes a visual distraction.

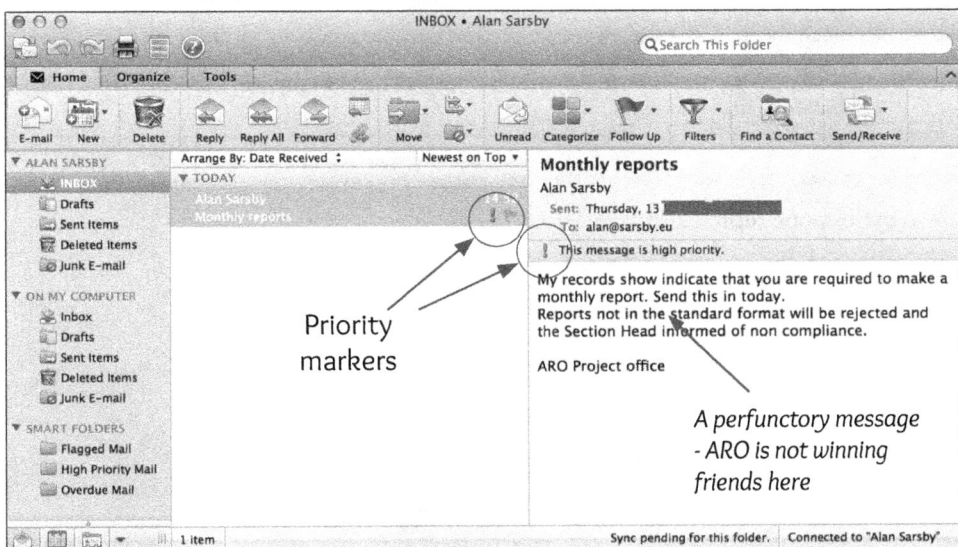

Priority markers

A perfunctory message - ARO is not winning friends here

The rule of thumb for priority is to leave it set at Normal. If the message really is urgent, say so in the subject line and in the main message.

If it is really very urgent, use the telephone instead and, if it is even more important, go to their office and speak with each other.

10.3.2. Read receipts

Some email systems have a feature known as Read Receipt. The idea is that you send a message and, once the recipient has opened the message, you receive a 'receipt' that records the message has been read.
This is just another form of 'cover your back.'

From the recipient's perspective, it can be really annoying to receive these. The recipient is presented with a dialogue box stating that a read receipt is going to be sent back to the originator. This has two unfortunate side effects:

It adds hassle to processing the Inbox.

It labels you, the sender, as someone who is 'covering their back' and puts your reputation at risk.

The read receipt generally only works within a closed email domain, for example, within your organisation. It doesn't always work across email domains. It is often disabled by IT support because there are security concerns.

> Note — Spammers use the read receipt mechanism to validate an email address.
> Spammers sell email address by the thousand, and their selling price is higher for validated email addresses.

In the screenshot following, un-tick the read receipts box.
Leave Importance set to Normal.

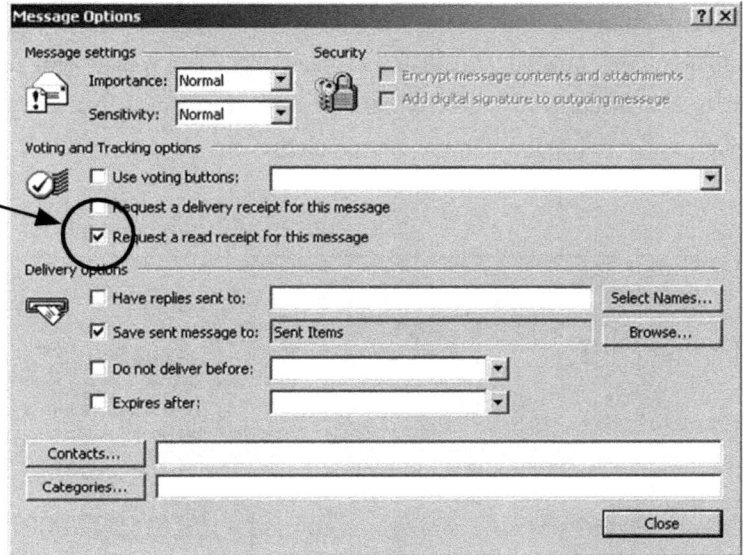

Turn off Read Receipt

Note — Many modern email programs no longer enable read receipts.
The screenshot above is from an earlier version.

10.4   Signatures and disclaimers

The final part of an email is the signature line.

Signatures convey useful information that might not be in the main message, for example, your job title or phone number. In keeping with the Postcard Principle, email signatures should be short and contain only essential information.

A good rule of thumb is to keep the signature line to fewer than 5 lines. Typically this would include, your name, role, phone number(s), web site, and a marketing strapline. This rule of thumb is difficult to achieve.

Emails in a business context often include legal element, for example disclaimers and (often wordy) policy statements. Additionally regulations require information such as the registered office and VAT registration to be included in business correspondence. All of which can make the signature lines quite lengthy.

It is becoming common to include graphics in a signature line, this can ease the space requirement, but keep in mind two problems. The first is that some recipients turn off images for security reasons. The second is that recipients can select to display emails as plain text and this doesn't show any graphics.

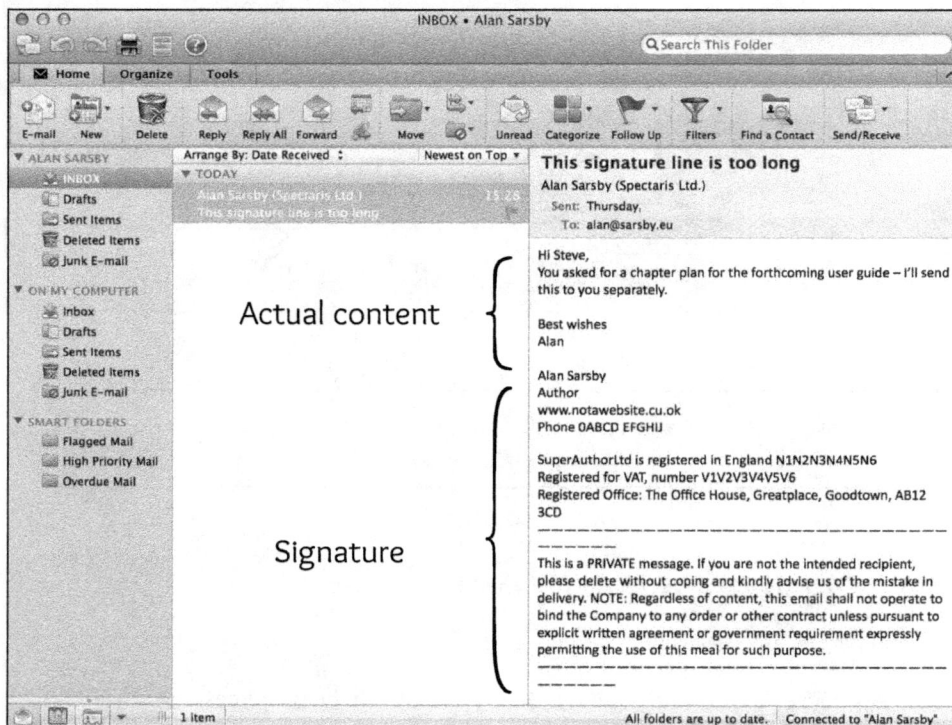

Desk Exercise

Just for fun, work out the ratio of message-to--signature above.

11 Before you send — Checklist

This checklist covers the main points that help you create an email that is a delight to receive. Remember each email you send carries your personal and professional reputation. it is worth spending a few moments to get it right!

- Why have you written this email?

- Is there a purpose to your email?

- Subject Line

- Does it have an inspiring and relevant subject line?

- Is there value to the recipient in the first few words?

- The main message

- Does the main message follow the Postcard Principle?

- Does it follow the one email, one topic rule?

- Does it start with a synchronisation?

- Is it scannable, using sub-headings and bullet points?

- Is the main message clear and concise?

- Have you used common fonts?

Addressing the email

- Is it addressed to the *fewest* number of recipients?

- Have you checked you're sending it to the right people?

- Are the addresses in the correct fields? (to: cc: and bcc:)

Signature

Is the signature as *short* as it can be?

Finally

Before you press Send, have you read the entire message out aloud?

For important emails, have you asked a colleague to proof read
or even better, *proof-speak* your message?

12 Put your inbox on a diet

12.1 How many emails?

Let's assume that you are a busy person — hmm, who isn't? Assume that you receive 25 emails each day. At the end of the week you might have 125 emails in your Inbox. That's about 500 per month. After a few months your Inbox becomes a bloated heap of messages with no relation to each other. And because finding specific messages is now difficult, you're becoming stressed.

There are several approaches to taking control of your Inbox:

Prevention at source

Get fewer emails sent to you. Make it known that you don't want the office gossip, or jokes, or copy-me-in (cover your back) messages.

Delete emails quickly

Develop a habit of deleting more often, more quickly, and automatically. Four tactics are:

- See and Delete — press delete without opening.
  (Think back to the value of a great subject line.)

- Read, react, and delete.
  (A well written and scannable message helps.)

- Move emails automatically to the deleted items folder without reading them first (they never show up in your Inbox).

Move emails out of your Inbox.

An unsorted Inbox quickly turns into a compost heap of messages; move them into specific folders.

- Read and then move the message to a folder. React later.

- Move the message to a folder using a Rule, and then read and react later.

Desk exercise

Find out how many emails you received in the previous month. it is likely that you'll discover the 500 emails mentioned above is an underestimate!

Assume that each email takes an average of 2½ minutes to process. Those 500 emails become 1250 minutes, or about 21 hours.

> That's <u>half a week per month</u>, just *'doing'* emails, rather than doing work!

In the busy world of corporate email, you don't have time for extended reading of emails. To reduce our email-driven workload, one needs to be both organised and disciplined.

12.2   Prevention at source

There are two main sources of excess emails:

Emails that you ask for or invite

These include newsletters, monthly updates, and similar bulk-mail messages. Other emails you might explicitly invite include normal business activities. This is also a consequence of your e-management style.

Emails that you don't ask for

These include proper and legitimate uses of email. But, once again, there is a cultural and e-management issue; it might be the norm in your organisation to forward the jokes and cute emails. But you own your Inbox. Let it be known you don't want these time wasters.

Let's start with those newsletters. If you've ever purchased something from a web-store, you'll have seen a link along the lines of *Sign-up for our daily newsletter*. It is ever so tempting to sign-up for these, receiving exciting, fresh new emails about something interesting. Except: you only need to sign up for a few of these newsletters and your Inbox starts to put on weight. Those newsletters soon add up, maybe to hundreds of unnecessary emails each month.

To reduce the quantity of newsletter emails:

Be very selective about signing up for newsletters.
You should check the originator's privacy policy. Double-check those tick boxes. By default, are you opting-in, or opting-out?

Be very cautious about entering competitions. Often the small print requires your email and an assumed opt-in to receive messages from 'carefully selected partner companies'. For the most part, you're inviting unsolicited emails.
One further thought — should you be entering competitions using your official business email? It depends on your organisation's email policy.

Unsubscribe from those newsletters that have long since served their purpose. For those messages that don't have an unsubscribe link, use a rule to move them directly to the Trash or Deleted Items folder.

12.3   Delete emails quickly — the power of the delete key

It is time to be ruthless, and your new best friend is the delete key. It is our first line of attack when pruning the oversized Inbox.

Delete without opening
If this seems harsh, remember that you can make a decision without opening the email. If it is clear from the subject line, or sender, that the message is of no value to you; press the delete key!

Open, read, then delete
Many emails are just for information, and often have a time-limited value. These don't need to be saved or filed, so just read and delete.

If **you need to reply, either:**

Do it immediately
If you can process the email in a few moments, then action it immediately. Make your reply, press send, then press delete.
Additionally, if your email system has the "after sending move to" facility, set it so the sent message is moved to the deleted items folder.

Move the message
Move the original message to a folder where you can deal with it later.

Delete automatically

You'll find that some messages just keep coming no matter how you try to prevent them. There is a method in most email programs to automatically delete messages so they never end up in your Inbox. But to make use of this feature, we need to understand the concepts of Folders, and Rules.

A short story:

A senior manager has a way of dealing with the 2000 emails that are in her Inbox when she comes back from her annual vacation. It is simple: Once the server has downloaded all the messages, she selects (clicks) the first message in the Inbox, presses Control-A (on a Windows PC)/Command-A (on a Mac) to select all the messages.

And then, you guessed it, presses the delete key. All gone!

It is an interesting e-management style; the assumption being if it is important, the originator sends it again. She's done this now for several years. She still has her job; and widely regarded as a productive and effective manager.

Maybe this isn't a best practice, and a scan might show a few important messages. However, there's no doubt that she is in control of her Inbox, not the other way around.

12.4   Using folders

For the most part, folders in email systems are just like folders in your computer's operating system. However, some folders have pre-designated purposes. For example, the Inbox is a folder to which all incoming messages are routed. The Sent Items folder is where a copy of the outgoing message is put after it is sent. The Deleted Items folder is where emails are put when you delete them. (The deleted items are not actually deleted; the deleted items folder is just in the email equivalent of the wastebasket. The Deleted Items folder can be emptied manually — typically using the Empty Deleted Items command — or automatically, at predefined intervals, (or when you quit the email program, this is usually a preferences choice.)

You can create folders for your own needs, for example projects, key activities, or people.

In the example following, there are folders for projects and folders for people. You might create a folder per project, and subfolders for the key parts. If you are a manager of others, a useful folder is 'Team'. Subfolders might then be for each team member, or for the monthly team meetings.

You can create a Read Later folder to put the interesting, but not important messages to read at leisure.

You can create as many folders as you choose that help with your job. What you can put in a folder varies. Each email program is different. All can hold email messages; some can hold notes, or files. You'll need to verify this yourself.

Using email folders is good way to become organised.

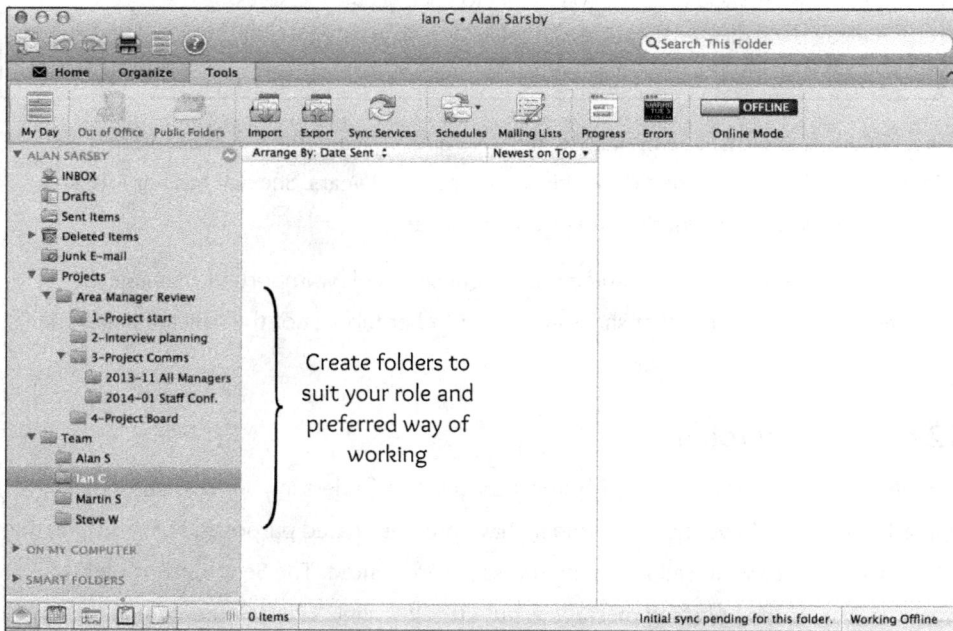

12.5   Automatic organisation using rules

12.5.1. Introducing rules

Modern email systems have a useful feature known as Rules. A Rule is a logical script that looks out for defined conditions in the incoming emails, and then carries out specific actions.

The logic of rules is based on the sequence: **If** 'something': **Then** 'carry out an action'.

A typical rule might be:

> **If** I get an email,
>> with the subject line *'monthly report'*

> **Then** move the email,
>> to the folder 'monthly reports'

Remember — inform your team to use the phrase 'monthly report' in their subject line.

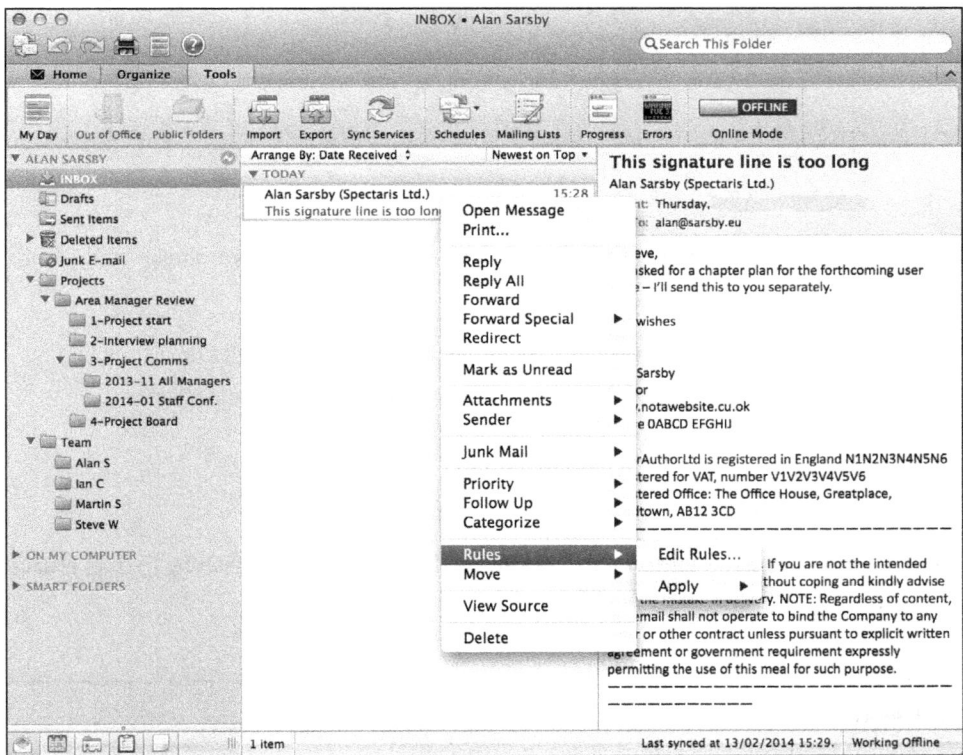

Using rules is a powerful way of keeping your Inbox slim by moving incoming messages directly to folders.

Rules can be created in many different ways, and it depends on which email program you are running.

Rules can be created directly from the main menu, or from inside the email. A common method is to right-click on the name of an incoming message and select Create Rule from the drop-down list.

There are other ways of accessing the Create Rule function, usually in a Tools menu; it depends on your email program.

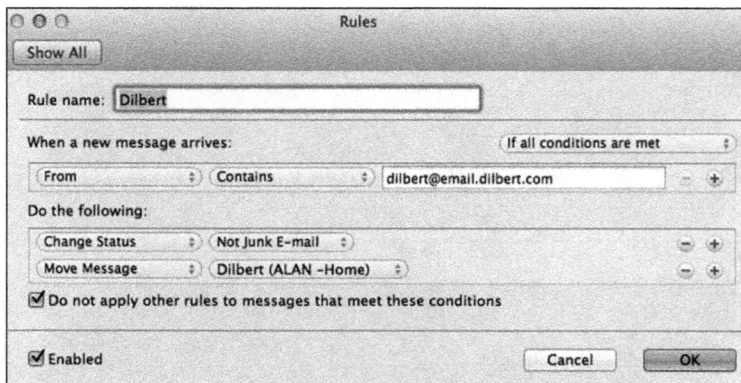

Following the dropdown menu to Create Rule presents a dialogue box similar to the one above.

From here, click the appropriate check boxes, fill in the details, and the next time you receive a message with those details, the *Do the following* actions are performed.

12.6   Automatically deleting emails

Let's be a bit more adventurous with rules and fulfil the promise of deleting certain emails automatically.

> **A short story:**
> The CEO of a large organisation was concerned about the amount of mail he was getting. Much of it was a *'cover your back'* style of message. The CEO let it be known that the emails which required action or intervention must be sent to him using the 'to' field. Any emails sent to the to him using the 'cc' field would be automatically deleted. This is more of leading by example, rather than a company wide policy, and as the CEO he could do this!

This automatic deletion was achieved using an email rule.

The logic is:

> **If** I get an email,
>> and I am in the cc list;
>
> **Then** move the email,
>> to the deleted items folder.

The screenshot below shows the detail of how this is achieved.

1   The rule is given a name 'CC to Trash'

2   The If section has one criterion:
     If any Cc recipient: contains boss@somewhare.kom

3   The **Then** section has one action:
     Move [the] message to Deleted Items (on my Computer).

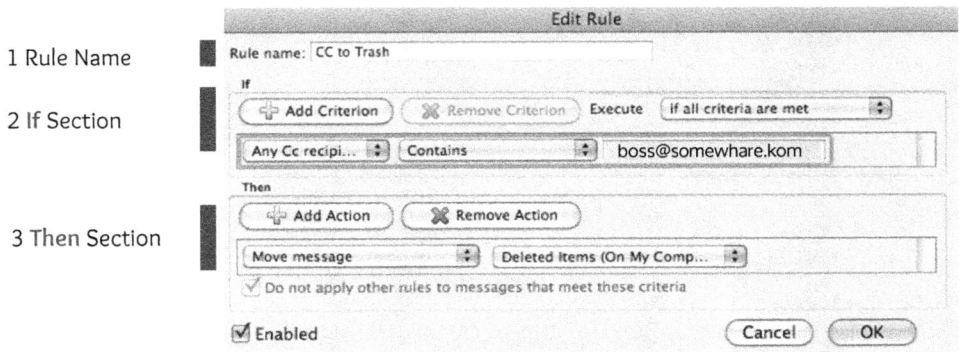

	Edit Rule
1 Rule Name	Rule name: CC to Trash
2 If Section	If — Add Criterion Remove Criterion Execute if all criteria are met — Any Cc recipi... Contains boss@somewhare.kom
3 Then Section	Then — Add Action Remove Action — Move message Deleted Items (On My Comp... ✓ Do not apply other rules to messages that meet these criteria
	☑ Enabled Cancel OK

> Remember the deleted items folder is just a folder like any other.
> Messages do not need to go via your Inbox at all.

12.7   Multi-criteria rules

Rules can have multiple criteria. You can create a single rule to intercept all the low priority messages (for example, the newsgroups), and move them to a 'Trash' folder.

In the following example, four different criteria are intercepted and the message is moved directly to the Trash folder without passing the Inbox.

1   The rule is given a name 'Instant Delete'

2   The **If** section has four criteria:

   - If 'Subject': contains 'computer problem'; OR

   - If 'From': contains: 'Help@ausergroup.cu.ok'; OR

   - is identified as 'Junk E-Mail'; OR

   - 'is from a mailing list'

3   The **Then** section has one action:
     Move the message to the folder 'Trash'.

A rule such as this can save enormous amounts of time, and make scanning your Inbox much easier.

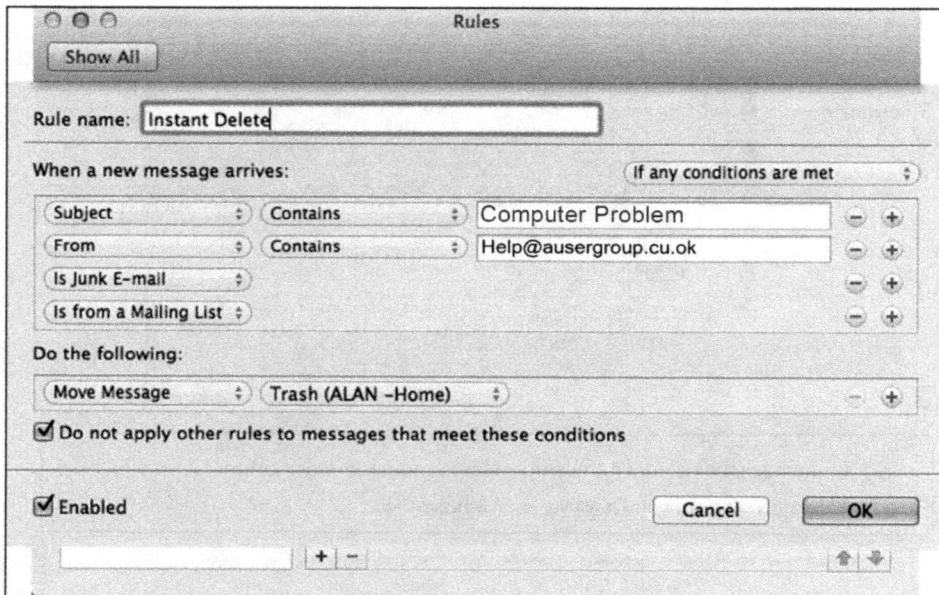

In the example above there is an **OR** element to the logic. This means if something OR something else OR something else again, is true, then do the action. So, whichever occurs first in the rule, the action is performed.

The OR is made to happen by selecting 'if any criteria are met' in the drop down menu.

Alternatively, logic can utilise AND elements. For example, if something AND something else AND something else again, are each true (so that everything in the criteria is true), THEN do the action. In this case, the drop down should be set to 'if ALL criteria are met'.

An important note about logic

It is best to keep your logic simple by expressing the **If** section as positive statements and restraining yourself to the two main operators of OR and AND.

> Note — You might be familiar with Boolean searches in search engines that use the **OR** and **AND** operators. The other logic operators are **NOT**, **NAND**, **NOR** and **XOR**. If you're not familiar with the mathematics of logic (Boolean algebra, De Morgan's Laws, and Karnaugh maps) your Rule might give strange results; hence the suggestion to keep it simple.

12.8   Delete the attachments – keep the email

In a corporate environment, it is likely that you'll have a quota for the size of your mailbox. Attachments can use up a great deal of space and can cause you to exceed your quota, perhaps with relatively few emails.

The attachments can be deleted from the email, without deleting the email. This leaves you free to save the textual part of the email in a suitable folder, and keep the attached file in your normal folders.

Usually, you can drag-and-drop the attachment to your desktop or to a folder in your operating system. Alternatively, there is often a function in the menus to save messages to your disk.

> Notes
>> When an attachment is added to an email, the size of the attachment increases by about one-third? This is normal to convert the attachment into a form that can be correctly transmitted across many networks. The file is restored to its proper size when the recipient saves it to disk.

12.9   Summary: managing your incoming mail

The power of deleting and the effectiveness of moving emails out of the Inbox to a specific folder: the thinking process is summarised below:

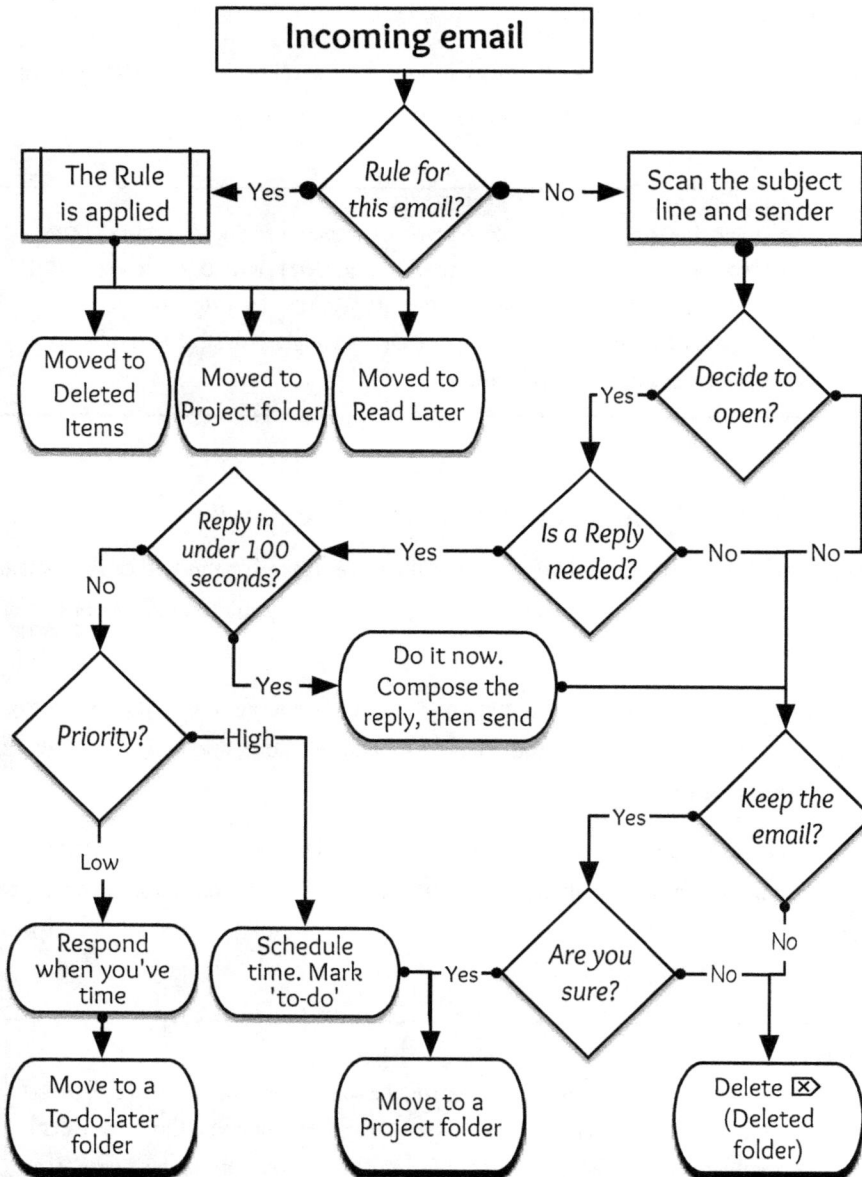

```
                        ┌─────────────────────┐
                        │   Incoming email    │
                        └─────────────────────┘
                                  │
                                  ▼
┌──────────────┐            ◇ Rule for ◇           ┌──────────────────┐
│  The Rule    │◄── Yes ──  ◇ this email? ◇ ── No ►│ Scan the subject │
│  is applied  │            ◇              ◇        │ line and sender  │
└──────────────┘                                   └──────────────────┘
       │                                                    │
       ├──────────┬──────────┐                              ▼
       ▼          ▼          ▼                       ◇ Decide to ◇
  Moved to    Moved to    Moved to        Yes ──     ◇   open?   ◇
  Deleted     Project     Read Later                 ◇          ◇
  Items       folder                                   │        │
                                                      No       No
              ◇ Reply in ◇                             │
   No ── ◇ under 100 ◇ ◄── Yes ── ◇ Is a Reply ◇ ── No ┘
          ◇ seconds? ◇            ◇  needed?   ◇
            │      │
            │     Yes ─►  Do it now.
            ▼            Compose the
        ◇ Priority? ◇    reply, then send
        ◇           ◇ ── High ─┐
            │                  │              ◇ Keep the ◇
           Low                 │     Yes ──   ◇  email?  ◇
            │                  │                │       │
            ▼                  ▼               No       No
       Respond          Schedule         ◇ Are you ◇
       when you've      time. Mark  ── Yes ── ◇  sure? ◇ ── No
       time             'to-do'
            │                  │
            ▼                  ▼                              ▼
       Move to a        Move to a                       Delete ⊠
       To-do-later      Project folder                  (Deleted
       folder                                           folder)
```

13 Your e-management style

13.1   Email is addictive

We mentioned that email is everywhere. It has invaded most areas of communications, and in a typical office, email is the first application opened at the beginning of the day, and usually stays active for the whole day. Your email is on hot standby, ready and waiting to interrupt you.

Email can be addictive in the same way that gambling is. We're excited by the possibility of receiving an unexpected prize. In email, the equivalent is an exciting email amongst all the dross, and this drives email addicts to check their email constantly. The sad fact is that email becomes the object of our endeavours rather than the support for our endeavours. For example, on our training courses, the most often mentioned time-waster is "doing emails".

Are you addicted?
Just for fun, try this *'am I addicted'* quiz:

- Did you check email less than 15 minutes ago?

- Is your email application permanently active?

- Do you respond to the incoming email notifications?

- Do you process each email as it comes in?

- Do you detach yourself from a conversation with a colleague to check an incoming email?

- Do you take a laptop or mobile phone into meetings to check emails during the breaks (or during uninteresting agenda items in a meeting)?

- Do you check for emails before your morning coffee?

- Do you check emails as soon as you arrive home from the office?

If you're answering more 'yes' than 'no' it is possible you have a level of addiction. In this section we'll look at how your habits affect your own performance, and how your habits affect others, especially if you lead a team.

13.2   Managing yourself

The cost of interruptions.

If you're addicted to emails, you might think *so what?* Isn't that normal in a business environment? Well, say you're working on a spreadsheet, and you interrupt yourself every 10 minutes to check emails. Or equally, you accept the interruption of incoming emails every time you hear the notification sound, (ker-ting, (and annoying in an open plan office) or see the notification slip into your working screen. When you return your attention to the spreadsheet it takes, typically, two-to-three minutes to regain your train of thought. For complex tasks it can take even longer.

Doing the arithmetic leads to some frightening messages:

> 2 minutes × 6 times per hour × 7 hours per day.

That's more than an hour, possibly two, *per day* in lost productivity.

The solution is to realise there's no need to be constantly checking emails. It is a habit, or behaviour, and it can be overcome. Some suggestions:

Take yourself off the network

The always-on, always present email is a cause of interruptions. Quit your email application, and only activate it at specific times in your day. Find a schedule that matches your workstyle. Accessing email in the early morning might be a good idea because some messages could contribute to your to-do list. Midday is also a good time. Try not to check emails in the final moments of your day; it is too late to take action. Avoid the stress and go home.

Turn off the email notifications

Reacting to the incoming email notification is inviting an interruption. Turn it off. Better still close or quit your email application.

Do emails between other tasks

In a typical working day, we all do a variety of tasks. Concentrate on one task, and when finished, check your emails. Then turn email off. Move on to the next task. Finish it. Check email. Turn email off.

Use the phone more often

There are many occasions when it is better to talk.

Invite fewer emails

We've mentioned the need for reduced emails and how to use rules to move some emails directly to the Deleted Items folder. There's also a behavioural aspect to fewer emails, and we'll devote a whole section to it in a moment.

Do lunch without email

Take time to recharge yourself. Try not to take your smart phone to lunch and 'do emails' whilst eating. Similarly, don't do work emails at weekends, and definitely not whilst on vacation.

Avoid the **self-justification** of *"it's the only time I get to do emails"* [3]

13.3   Please drown me in CCs

In larger organisations there is often a culture of covering your back. Including people in the cc list achieves this. Earlier we told the story of the CEO who automatically deletes cc'd messages without reading them. This is the other side to the story:

Let's say that you've asked your team members to *"copy me in, just to keep me informed."* It sounds ever so reasonable and innocent; you might think that you are empowering the team to get on with things, but it doesn't scale.

A little arithmetic demonstrates the problem:

> Say your team member sends an email to 3 people, and copies you in. At this point you have 1 extra message in your Inbox.
>
> The 3 people each respond with 'Reply All.'
> You now have 4 emails.
>
> If your team member sends 5 emails per day like this,
> you now have 20 emails.
>
> If your team is 5 people, all behaving like this, your Inbox is attracting 100 emails per day, or about 500 per week.

The reason you have 500 extra emails in your Inbox is because *you asked for them!* Re-do the 2½ minutes exercise and we have another 21 hours of lost productivity!

---

3   If you find that the use self-justifications is your normal practice, it is time to seek some management development training.

It gets worse. Let's say that one of the recipient's notices that you, as the team leader, have been copied in, and in order to maintain parity of rank, adds their own boss to the cc list. This escalation creates even more emails. It is unsustainable.
You are drowning in a self-generated storm of emails.

The example is not extreme. It is an underlying cause of people *'doing emails'* instead of *'doing work'*. Sadly this is of our own making!

Your reputation is also at risk. With all those cc'd emails flying about you are advertising yourself as a control freak, micromanager, or as someone who doesn't trust their staff. If this applies to you, consider some management development or get a mentor.

If you really do need to cover your back, do it outside the email exchanges.

13.4   Managing others — are you e-stealing peoples' time?

The assumption is that email is a near-instantaneous messaging medium; you press send, and a moment later it is in the recipient's Inbox. The illusion is that it is a phone call without the speaking part! This has changed some aspects of management behaviour.

Demanding instant replies
In the past, a message asking for thoughts might give adequate notice, but now, it is common to see a demand along the lines of *"let me have your input by 5pm."*

And just as bad is sending an email, then phoning the recipient a few moments later to check if they've read it!

Mail and run delegation
Simply forwarding a message to a colleague as a way of delegating a task might be simple and easy for you, but not if it bypasses the normal management skills of delegation.

Management by emailing about
Management by *walking* around is generally considered a good idea. It is good to be seen around the office, and good to be approachable. The nonverbal clues in a real encounter indicate what kind of response is expected. It might be a short chat or the need to book some time in the diary; it is not the same with email.
A *'How's it going'* email contains little about what kind of response is expected. Is it

a subtle demand for a status report? A status report takes time to compose. You've just stolen your recipient's time.

ASAP

ASAP (As Soon As Possible) was created by an organisation that lives and breaths in abbreviations and acronyms — the military. ASAP wasn't a request, but a demand. As an instruction it relies on rank and positional authority. The General can ASAP the corporal, but not the other way around.

In everyday life, ASAP in emails has several problems:

- As a demanding/commanding imperative it labels you as a control freak. Bad for your reputation. (And almost as bad is JFDI[4], or DIN[5])

- It is ambiguous. It could mean put the task on your to-do list and do it when you get around to it; or it could mean do-it-now. Once again, your recipient makes the choice, not you.

- It relies on a command-and-control relationship between the sender and receiver.

Take care with ASAP. Try not to use it.

13.5   Summary

Be aware that email can be addictive — if you let it.

Manage email as a specific task. Turn it off when email is not the task.

If you ask to be copied in just in case, be prepared to drown in a sea of emails. The lost productivity is substantial.

Don't cc someone in an email unless there is a very good reason for it. Make it clear in the message why they are cc'd.

Don't steal other people's time with your emails. Demanding ASAPs gives you a 'bad manager' reputation. Email is not a substitute for real management actions — seeing and speaking with your colleagues.

---

4   JFDI — Just Flipping Do It. This is the polite version, you can imagine the gritty industrial version.
5   DIN — Do It Now. (And JFDIN combines both with a much stronger tone!

14 Never use email for sensitive personnel tasks

Email provides the perfect excuse not to speak with people, and the ease by which emails can be sent helps us avoid speaking when we really should. If you are using email to avoid a difficult meeting, you're a management coward.

As a general rule, the more sensitive a message is, the less it is suited to email.

Conveying bad news.
Delivering bad news is a distinct facilitative skill. It only works in a private, face-to-face environment where the conversation can proceed a bit at a time, and the participants can pick up visual clues from each other. Email is not that medium.

Criticism and negative feedback
Email is good for praise and not good for criticism. Although hopefully, you'd never criticise anyway, a coaching style always gets better results. Coaching needs a real conversation to make it work. Use the phone instead.

Private and personal
Private details such as pay, promotion, often requires a written/signed paper to be legal, and so might not be suitable for an email. Before you send this kind of information as an email, speak with the individual to set their expectations. And validate the action with your Human Resources or Legal departments.

Feelings and feedback
Imagine that a colleague has asked for feedback from an unsuccessful interview. Feelings and emotions are running high, and these can be difficult meetings to manage. This kind of meeting needs distinctive skills and approaches that cannot be achieved by email. Using email for this denies the recipient the opportunity to ask questions, understand, and learn from the feedback.

Confidential information
There are so many different forms of confidential, it is impossible to generalise. Remember once you've pressed Send, you've effectively published it.

15 A skilful reply

15.1   Get ready

By now, we have sorted or deleted incoming emails. The Inbox is slim and those emails that need further thought are safely in their respective folders. It is time to look at those that needed further thought and a reply.

We can reuse those 5 Ws and 1 H to create a skilful and business like reply.

- Why reply
- When to reply
- Who to reply to
- What is the reply
- How to reply
- Where to compose the reply

15.2   Why reply

The first step in a skilful reply is to decide whether a reply is really needed. What is the purpose in replying?

You might have been asked a specific question, in which case the purpose is to provide the answer. Obvious really. But it is not always clear-cut and taking a moment to use the Know, Think, Do method helps you be clear about investing valuable time in the reply.

Remember you don't always have to reply. You have choices — keep it or delete it; use the phone, or walk to their desk.

Always give thought to the purpose of the reply.

15.3   When to reply

There are two aspects to 'when'.

The time management aspect

Timeliness is important in all forms of communication. So when you reply is a balancing act between importance, urgency, and your own time. This comes down to time management and prioritising.

If you do choose to reply later, and later is sometime off, a holding reply reassures your recipient that you're not ignoring their message.

Your personal state

There are times when we are all stressed, and the content of some emails make us angry. That's life. As a rule of thumb:

- Try not to rush a reply.
  Rushed replies encourage mistakes. This is another reason why it is not a good idea to check your emails just before you leave work.

- Never reply to an email if you are angry.
  Take a deep breath and reply later.

15.4   Who to reply to

How many people should your reply be sent to? To the fewest necessary.

If in doubt, reply to the sender only. If you see a long list of addressees, take a moment to think about who really needs to see your reply. Consider:

- Reply to sender only

- Reduce the number of reply-to addresses. (Think back to the copy-me-in problem.)

- Never use the Reply All option unless you have a need for it.

> A short story (with names changed to protect the guilty)
>   Sue emailed everyone in her team to say she was leaving. Jill got the job of organising the leaving card and surprise present. Jill emailed everyone to say she was organising things and a suggested amount for a surprise present.
>   Except that it wasn't a surprise to Sue, because Jill clicked the Reply All button. So Sue knew all about the 'surprise'.

15.5   Replies that are a delight to receive

The reply should be one that the recipient looks forward to reading! Use the clarity toolkit from earlier to craft a good reply. Even if the incoming email was poor, you can lead by example by sending a good reply (and elevating your reputation along the way). Try to compose the reply as a stand-alone message with synchronisation, message, and signature.

There's an additional aspect of the reply — it is quoting. When you click reply, most email applications take a copy of the incoming message and put this at the bottom of the new message ready for you to type the response. How this looks depends on your particular email system. It could be indented and put in a different colour, or for plain text messages each line of the incoming message is prefixed with a quoting character, usually a chevron (>). This depends on your email application and how it has been configured.

Including the incoming message is helpful because it reminds the sender what they wrote and reinforces the context and purpose of your reply. However, after a couple of exchanges in an email conversation, the quantity of quoted text becomes large compared to the new text. it is good practice (in most circumstances) to remove excess quoting. The commonly accepted indicator that text has been removed is the [snip] signal. To use this, simply select the quoted text that's not needed, and replace it with [snip] — this indicates that some text has been removed — snipped out.

Sometimes, an incoming message has several questions that each needs only a short reply from you. In these cases it is generally acceptable to reply within the quoted text. Even so, your response should start with a synchronisation that points the reader to the quoted text. Remember your job is to make it easy for the receiver, so use [snip] and delete to compress the original, now quoted, text to the minimum needed.

15.6   How to reply — perhaps not by email

Earlier, we discussed several examples where an email is the wrong medium for certain messages. Try not to let the quick and easy method of pressing 'Reply' lull you into situations where using the phone would be better.

15.7   Where to reply

The 'where' aspect of the 5Ws might seem odd. However, emails can be sent from your desk pc, your mobile phone, and tablet, almost everywhere on many devices.

It might be easy to prune your Inbox on the train — quick scans and the ever-useful delete key, but it is not the place to work on confidential messages. On the other hand, the advantage of the train is to use it as thinking time, perhaps to think about the more difficult messages. Alternatively, you could close your eyes and use the journey to recharge your batteries so you arrive at work ready for the day.

15.8   Forwarding

There is often a need to forward the email to someone who wasn't on the original distribution.

A professional way to forward emails is to explain why you think it important to forward the message, to mention the original sender in the text, and to include the original sender in the cc list. it is also a good idea to delete [snip] and generally tidy up the message to make it relevant to the new recipient.

The dark side of forwarding is that it can attract the same trouble as bcc messages. You must have a real reason for forwarding.

15.9   Summary – before you press send

- Is there a need or purpose to reply?

- Should you use the telephone instead?

- Reply to the fewest possible people.

- Double-check the 'to' and 'cc' fields to verify who you are sending the email to.

- Reply All can be hazardous — try not to use it.

- Write the reply so that the originator looks forward to receiving it.

- Forwarding — say why — remove source addresses — clean up first.

- Move the sent message to a specific folder, or delete it. Don't leaving it cluttering up your Sent Items folder.

16 The postcard principle, part 2

We introduced the postcard principle earlier as a way of limiting the quantity of text that should be in an email. From this principle we developed the clarity toolkit to craft short and unambiguous emails.

We've hinted a few of times now, that there is a second aspect of the postcard principle. You might have heard the old adage:

> *Never write something on a postcard you don't want the others to read.*

Everyone who handles a postcard has the opportunity to read it. To put this the other way around — never write anything in an email that you wouldn't put on a postcard. Emails are postcards. Postcards are not private. Email is not private. With a few clicks your badly worded message can be seen by everyone in the world. Leaked emails are a fact of life in politics. Leaked emails tell the competition what you're doing.

Snottograms (emails with an ill-mannered, angry, or sarcastic message) end up in unexpected places. This example (July 2011) is a news report concerning a future Mother-in-Law giving her future Daughter-in-Law some 'advice' on social etiquette.
See: www.bbc.co.uk/newsbeat/13973278

Once again:
Never write anything in an email that you wouldn't put on a postcard.

There is an extra side to this non-private nature of emails. Your employer may be monitoring your email messages. Whatever you send may be silently copied to someone who has the job of watching what you say. This is legitimate — it is often needed to ensure compliance with company policies.

Never write
anything in an
email that you
wouldn't put on
a postcard!

Great
Emails

Leadership
Library

To:
a.reader@connexion.kom

17 Attachments

17.1 Benefits and curses

Attachments are both a benefit and a curse. Attachments can be almost anything — images, presentations, or working documents. On the other hand, attachments can be a nuisance to the receiver, especially if they are large, unwanted, or worse, cannot be opened.

17.2 Adding attachments

An attachment is another file, such as a document, spreadsheet, or presentation, which is attached to your message. Compare this with an old-style letter: the envelope would have a covering letter, and some enclosures. Attachments is the the same as postal-mail's enclosures.

Is the attachment necessary?

Check that you have a real purpose in using an attachment.

An attachment that contains just a few sentences places an extra burden on your recipient. Would it be more effective to put the text in body of the email?

Use a commonly understood format

For example — Microsoft Office documents (.doc, .docx, .xls, .ppt). Portable documents, .pdf. Adobe Creative Suite/Cloud documents (.psd, .ai, indd). Industry standard files, including .jpeg/jpg for images, .mp3/.mp4/.aiff files for sound, .rtfd/rtf for word processor documents, and so on. The golden rule is to be sure your reader can open the file. If in doubt, ask.

Can the attachment be delivered by other means?

Rather than attaching large files, can the attachment be delivered another way? For example: as a link in your email (if permitted in your environment), through a web portal, or through a corporate collaboration system (Instant Messaging, Skype, iChat, and MSN) also support file transfer.

Keep the attachments small

Modern email systems can handle large attached files. Up to 10Mbytes or more is usual. But some don't. If you have a batch of large files, send them one at a time in separate emails. Or use links. Remember, the size of the attachment increases one-third for transmission via email.

Don't attach application programs

Application files, for example, .exe, .com, and .app, and others, are very dangerous to send to others. The two reasons are

> **Potentially rouge software** — carrying out unwanted activities such as keystroke logging, deleting files, or what is now often called ransomware. (Your computer is taken over (kidnapped) and only restored on payment of the ransom.)

> **Legal and licensing** — Software is protected by copyright laws. By copying the program to others you leave yourself and your organisation open to legal action. If you are in a corporate environment, it is likely that your IT services block these.

Don't attach unusual files

For example, if you attach a folder, some email clients automatically create an archive (for example a .zip file) but others don't.

Don't attach confidential files

If the content is confidential, simple attachments are risky. Some common formats carry a great deal of metadata that can betray confidentiality. More about this in the Appendixes.

17.3   Safe and dangerous attachments

The previous section dealt with sending attachments, this section deals with receiving attachments.

You've received an email with an attachment. Now what? Should you open it, delete, or ignore it? Why should you be bothered?
Attachments are one of the easiest ways to spread computer viruses, hoaxes, Trojans and other malware. Each of these are subtly different but can cause a lot of trouble.

Some attachments are safe to open and others definitely not safe. However, it is simply impossible to produce a definitive safe list.

Staying safe with attachments depends on your own caution and common sense, so the way to proceed is by using a kind of triage for emails.

Do you know the sender?

Is the message with the attachment from someone you know and trust? This element of common sense works both ways.

For example, if a team member sends you an attachment, say a file called `'budget-2018.xls'` — it could be that you were already expecting the file and it is normal. (See below regarding Macros.)

For example, you receive an email from someone you know who forwards all those cutesy emails with strange attachments. You can use one of the delete tactics using rules, then send a short message, or pick up the phone and mention you don't want this stuff!

Is the file a well-known type?

The table following indicates some safe and dangerous attachments. The remark above about a 'given value of safe' is especially true here.

Are you suspicious about the file?

Some mail systems (and computer operating systems) try to make your life easier by hiding the file extensions — the letters that follow the final dot, for example, *.doc* Find out how to turn this feature off. You'll then be able so see more about the attachment.

The files in the possibly dangerous column of the table shown on the next page should be treated with suspicion. A quick line of defence is to telephone the sender and find out what it is.

Your main line of defence is, you guessed it, the delete key.

Is the file asking for a password?

If you open the file and are prompted to enter a password, especially your logon or system password, the file is highly suspicious. Delete it.

But just to keep the balance in this section, some documents have password features, for example an Excel spreadsheet can be password protected. However you should know that it is coming. If you open a spreadsheet that unexpectedly asks you for a password, pick up the telephone and check with the originator. Otherwise, press Delete.

Has the attachment two extensions?

If a file has two extensions, for example `picture.jpg.exe` — it is an application trying to disguise itself as an image. Press the delete key.

One exception to this rule of thumb is when a file has been compressed. For example, a file called `financial_plan.xls.zip` is an Excel spreadsheet that has been compressed to produce a .zip file. Opening this kind of file normally de-compresses the file to leave you with the original.
But beware — if it was something like `financial_plan.exe.zip` — it is using the .zip extension to get past your defences. This is an application (and executable file, hence .exe) in disguise.
You know what to do — Delete!

A useful feature of Microsoft Office files is the ability to add your own features using a programming language known as Visual Basic. They can be included in documents (such as a spreadsheet) where they are known as Macros. Macros have been used to carry malware. Normally, applications warn you if the file contains a macro. It might be normal for your work, but if you're not expecting this to happen, treat the file as suspicious.

If you're working behind a corporate firewall, it is very likely that most emails are scanned as they arrive (and sent) and offending attachments are removed before they reach you. However, it is not an excuse to be lazy or to let down your guard.

Probably safe this is not a comprehensive list	Possibly dangerous this is not a comprehensive list

Still Image formats
    .bmp .jpeg .jpg .gif .tiff .tif .png
	Executable (application) files
	    .exe .com .app,.js .jse

Movie files
    .avi .mov .rm .mp4 .m4a, .wav .wma
	Operating system files
	    .cmd .ins .isp .ocx .pif .reg .scr .shs

Sound files
    .aiff, .mp3, mp4, .m4v .wav
	Scripting or automation files
	    .vbs .bat .vbs .vbe

Text and display files .txt .text .rtf .rtfd .pdf	Any file with a double extension
Web page attachments .htm .html .webarchive	.jpg.vbs

Industry standard files
    Adobe files
    .psd .ai .indd
	.txt.scr
	    .jpg.exe
	    .pdf.exe

Drawing files .dwg .vis .graffle	Links to other places

Apple files:
    .pages .numbers .key
	.lnk
	    .webloc

Microsoft files
    .doc .docx .dot .dotx .ppt .pptx .pps,
    .xls, .xlsx .vsd .mpc .mpp, and others.	

Note: There are thousands of file extensions. A useful resource is on
       Wikipedia en.wikipedia.org/wiki/Filename_extension.
       Alternatively use your favourite search engine to ascertain what you've been sent.

17.4   Summary — attachments

- Have you been cautious and considerate with attachments?

- Have you considered what metadata is in your attachments?

- Are you ready with the delete key?

18 Self defence for emails

18.1 The email jungle

The age of innocence in emails has long since passed. Our Inboxes have messages of dubious content. Some attempt to sell body-part enhancements, others are hoaxes, and some have sinister intent. This part of our guide is about staying safe in the potentially hostile e-world.

We look at two features that are helpful in their innocence, but best considered from a safety and security perspective. Then we look at the kind of emails that cause panic, some are pranks. Others have criminal intent.

18.2 Be cautious with out of office replies

Imagine you are a thief. You want to break into someone's house. What clues do you look for to be sure the occupants are not in? The householder forgot to cancel the milk, forgot to cancel the newspapers, and a lot of mail that you can see through the glass door. And the next-door neighbour simply tells you they are on vacation. Bingo. I'll come back later with the crowbar and glass cutter.

Have you thought that the same clues might be given to the thief by email?

The clues are delivered using a function usually known as out-of-office reply. When you activate an out of office function, it automatically responds to incoming messages, with a new email to a sender.

These out of office replies might be useful to let senders know that you cannot reply to their message. It prevents your contacts repeatedly sending you more and more messages, perhaps with an ever-escalating level of urgency.

But back to our thief, in the example of an out of office reply following, what might help you plan your burglary?

```
Hello, thanks for your message. I am on vacation, and
unable to access email until 16 September. For any
urgent enquiries please contact the Blackthorn Centre
on 01xxx abc nnn, or contact Mary, on 01xxx abc xyz.
Thanks.
```

It is a role-model out-of-office reply, it has most of the 5Ws and 1H, a date, and who to contact. So far so good, but:

If that out of office reply arrived back in my inbox and I was an unscrupulous individual or casually mentioned to someone else or it was overheard in a public place, I would now:

- Know you are on vacation.

- Think your house might be empty until 16 September.

- Telephone, Mary, and trick her into revealing extra details.

The out of office reply is also a way for spammers to validate your email address. The spammers took a guess at your address, for example combining popular first names with popular surnames and using your company or organisation domain, blasted hundreds of emails to it. A few of these pot shots are lucky and reach a real person. Then your auto reply confirms it. Your address becomes more valuable for sale to others, who then target you with more specific emails, possibly with criminal intent.

Creating a good out of office reply follows the same process as replying. The first step is having a purpose for an out of office reply. Let's assume that you have a reason; the out of office text needs to be clear and concise, but not necessarily complete.

For example:

```
Thank you for your message. I am not able to reply at
the moment. If you need an urgent response, please
call the support team on 01xxx abc xyz.
Best regards
```

Stay safe. If you need to use out of office replies, then:

- Do not state the dates of your absence and return date.

- Do not state that you are on holiday or out of the country.

- Do not include your home address or home telephone number.

- Do include another person to contact if the enquiry is urgent.

- Make sure that person is fully briefed in the security aspects.

To say it again, remember that automated out of office replies are effectively advertising who you are, what you do, and the circumstances of your absence. To fraudsters and burglars, your helpful and over informative out of office reply is a gift — or even an invitation.

You could use a Rule instead

There are situations when a reply is a desirable action; for example, important customers try to contact you whilst you're on vacation. Creating an email rule could be a better approach; for example, forwarding the incoming email from the important customer directly to a colleague. And of course you'll have briefed your colleague and your customer.

18.3   Turn off download pictures

The use of images in emails is now common especially in advertising messages. These emails use the same technology used to view a web page in a browser; it is a web page within an email.

The images can be self-contained within the email, or can be externally referenced.

It is the externally referenced images that can be dangerous. When you open the email, the image is brought in from an external web site. That image can be given a name that is unique to you, so as soon as the image is downloaded, the spammer knows you have a real email address. Your email address is sold and you become a target for spam, hoaxes, and malicious emails.

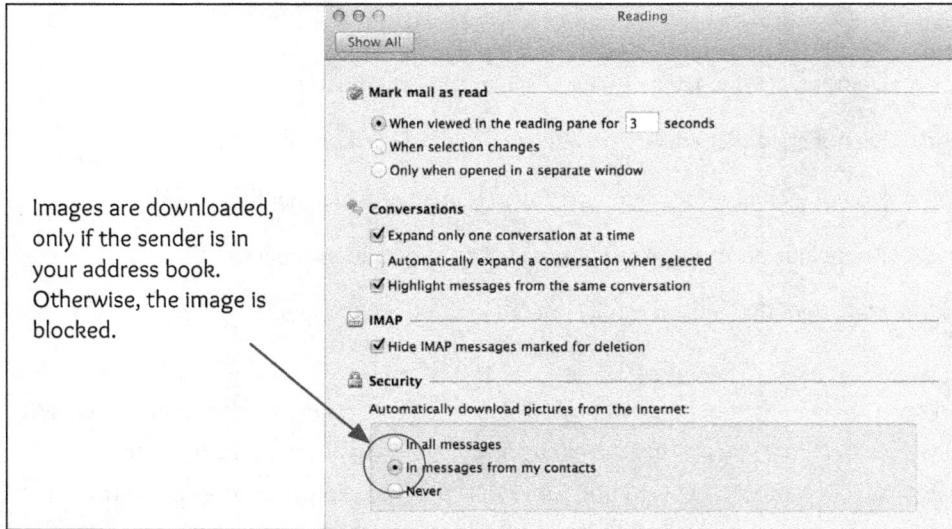

Images are downloaded, only if the sender is in your address book. Otherwise, the image is blocked.

Modern email applications include an option to turn off automatic downloads. Look in the preferences or the Tools-> Security settings to find this. In the example above, the checkbox referring to HTML[6] controls whether you see the plain text version of the incoming email (assuming it has one embedded in the message) or whether the web-page like email is displayed. You then have options for downloading pictures.

By turning off the download images, your email displays empty placeholder spaces instead of the picture. This gives you the chance to look at the message and decide whether to download the images or, you guessed it, press delete.

6   HTML – Hyper-Text Mark-up Language, is the underlying technology used to 'mark' text so that the browser knows what to do with it. This is the web page in an email mentioned earlier.

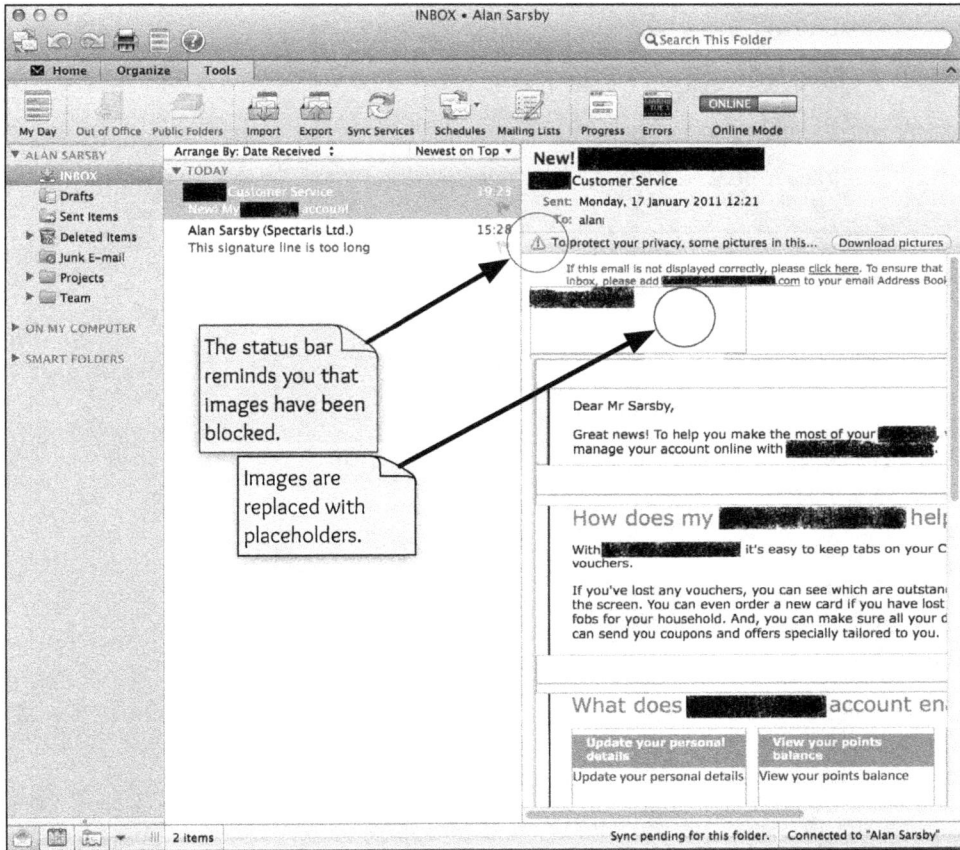

Turning off images is a useful security measure. In the example above, there is enough to help you decide whether you feel ok to download the images. Turning off images also saves space in your inbox.

19 Hoax, Scams, and Trojan emails

19.1 The hoax formula

Many hoaxes follow a formula. Once you're aware of the formula, it becomes easier to spot them, and press the delete key. A common five-part formula is:

- Outline a plausible scenario;

- Attribute it to an authoritative source;

- Create panic/anger/fear;

- Propose a magical set of actions to fix it;

- Tell everyone.

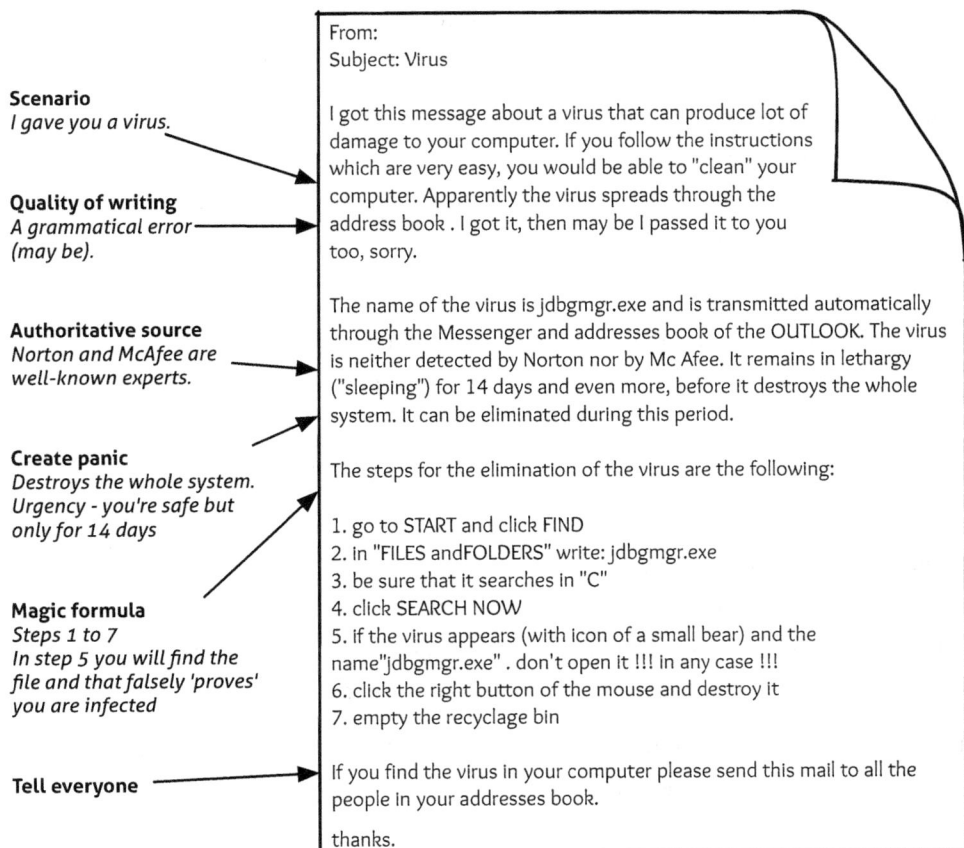

Scenario
I gave you a virus.

Quality of writing
A grammatical error (may be).

Authoritative source
Norton and McAfee are well-known experts.

Create panic
Destroys the whole system. Urgency - you're safe but only for 14 days

Magic formula
*Steps 1 to 7
In step 5 you will find the file and that falsely 'proves' you are infected*

Tell everyone

From:
Subject: Virus

I got this message about a virus that can produce lot of damage to your computer. If you follow the instructions which are very easy, you would be able to "clean" your computer. Apparently the virus spreads through the address book . I got it, then may be I passed it to you too, sorry.

The name of the virus is jdbgmgr.exe and is transmitted automatically through the Messenger and addresses book of the OUTLOOK. The virus is neither detected by Norton nor by Mc Afee. It remains in lethargy ("sleeping") for 14 days and even more, before it destroys the whole system. It can be eliminated during this period.

The steps for the elimination of the virus are the following:

1. go to START and click FIND
2. in "FILES andFOLDERS" write: jdbgmgr.exe
3. be sure that it searches in "C"
4. click SEARCH NOW
5. if the virus appears (with icon of a small bear) and the name"jdbgmgr.exe" . don't open it !!! in any case !!!
6. click the right button of the mouse and destroy it
7. empty the recycle bin

If you find the virus in your computer please send this mail to all the people in your addresses book.

thanks.

> Note — This example has been around since 2002 and still turns up.
>
> By the way, the file mentioned in the hoax, `jdbgmgr.exe` is a harmless file present on some Microsoft Windows operating systems. Software development software uses it.

It is worth taking a page to describe how this hoax works.

1. **Shock-horror**

   The hoax starts with *I've got a virus and you've got it too.* The goal of the hoax writer is to make you worry and create the conditions for panic. It is essential for what comes next...

2. **Consolidate the panic**

   Search for this file. You find it. That 'proves' you have the virus too. The panic sets in. Your rational processes are being shut down and you're in survival mode.

3. **Authoritative source**

   Two leading experts confirm your finding. More Panic. You've got the virus and your life's work is about to be destroyed. *Panic is now full on.*

4. **Magic action**

   But here is a magic thing you can do to fix it and everyone will be OK. In terror, you follow the instructions in the hope of being liberated from this tyranny. It works as described. Phew!

5. **Tell everyone**

   The tell everyone instructions comes with detailed instructions so that you're still trapped in this traumatic ordeal — in other words the virus writer has still psychologically got you by the throat and not letting rational thought get in the way. Without thinking, you follow the instructions, and you tell everyone.

At the end of this experience, you might be thinking you've just been rescued from an imminent disaster, and by doing the good deed of letting others know about the situation, you feel much better. Except that you've been the victim of a hoax and you've sent it on to all your friends, who then experience the horror of this hoax.

The authors of these chain-email hoaxes get their satisfaction from seeing their handiwork come back to them, often years later.

19.2   Put up your defences

Being alert and cautious is the way forward. Be sceptical:

Check the authoritative sources

you'll find they are vague and unnamed. Examples of 'authorities' are along the lines:

- this came from the British Computer Society ...

- a friend from the local police station ...

- the information arrived today from Microsoft ...

- AOL have confirmed the severity of ...

There won't be any substantive detail; nothing you could check or verify.

Does it follow a formula?

Another example is

- If you receive Life is beautiful.pps,

- don't open it,

- it deletes everything,

- We must do everything possible to stop it.

- Tell all your friends.

When you get a message that your life's work is about to be destroyed with virus, your actions should be:

- Restore your rational thinking — Take a moment to think
  Breathe deeply. Inspect the message; see it for what it is, then:

- Check for known hoaxes and virus — See the resources the Appendix.

- Do not tell everyone! Break the chain.

- Press delete. (You guessed that already?)

19.3   The phishing formula

A more sinister version of a hoax is known as phishing — as in fishing. The fishing is an attempt to catch some essential information, typically on-line banking details, such as login and passwords. Once the phisher has this information, the money in your account is stolen. Sadly, this is not a hoax and people fall for this trick.

A common formula is:

```
An urgent message from xyz Bank
(This is the authoritative source)

Your account has been compromised and suspended for
your own safety.
(The plausible scenario and threat —you cannot get
to your money.)

Follow this link to Log in and confirm your details.
(The magic solution to regain access to your money.)

The link takes you to a convincing fake web site and
you log in. The fake web site captures your log-in
details.
(Carry out the magic action.)

Your account is unlocked. Relief.
```

And then the phisher, now now in possession of your login details, logs in to your bank account and transfers (steals) your money.

The theft happens quickly, typically only a few moments later. If were any any longer, the phisher runs the risk that their victim might realise what was going on, and changed their password.

Another common example is shown below:

Scenario
Important subject line. Note the exclamation!

Salutation
A clue that the sender doesn't know your name, so they use your email address

Plausible scenario
Some changes to your account

A threat
service is to be interrupted

Magic formula
Confirm and update by Clicking here. Implied urgency by using **red**

Authoritative source
But note the spelling error 'Costumer'.

Extra detail
Extra detail to make it look genuine.

The real link
Hovering over the link, shows its true destination. It's not going to the bank, but to a fake located elsewhere *yazzcolor.cl*

Once you recognise the formula, it is easier to deal with these phishing emails.

Urgent message

The purpose of the 'urgency' is to tempt you to open the message. If you simply delete the message (always a good idea) the phisher has failed. So, these phishing messages have urgent elements to their subject line. Examples include *account suspended:* or *Urgent Notification:* or *Restore your Account Access: Errors on your internet bank account.*

Plausible scenario

Several scenarios are used by the phishers. Typical scenarios include *Unusual activity,* or *unable to verify:* And often a threat: *your account has been suspended.* A threat like this means you cannot use your money. Remember the purpose is to create panic so that you don't look too deeply at the critical phishing instructions.

A magic solution

The magic solution is a convenient link to the bank's web site. Where you can log in and verify your account. **Real banks never do this**.

Verify the link

In many email applications, hovering your cursor above a link reveals the link details. In the example above, the real destination is shown at the bottom of the pane. In this case to a domain registered in the Ivory Coast.

Remember: **Real banks never do this.**

19.4   Phishing defences

Spam and phishing messages are often intercepted by the email server and routed to a junk folder (or in some cases instantly deleted by the server before you ever see them).

However some get through, so the following summary offers a few clues to identifying phishing:

Checklist - phishing clues

Is the phishing email similar to others apparently coming from different sources? Lazy phishers use the same message but with different bank details in the hope of finding one that you have money in.

Does the salutation use your real name? If it is generic in any way, treat it as a fake.

Does the email offer a convenient link for you to follow? it is worth saying again — Real banks never do this. Real banks never ask for your login and security information like this. Don't follow links (disguised in images); always type the bank's web address directly into your browser.

Check the real underlying address of links — this is often shown in the status area of the email, or pops up in an alert box. Sometimes they are clever misspellings of a real institution. Be aware that these links can take you to a place where legal redress is not available.

The phishers make their fake web site look like the real thing.
If in doubt, don't.

Professionalism — the earlier example concerning the `jdbgmgr.exe` hoax has many errors — typos, grammar. Delete.

Is the email asking for your help as an intermediary? These often start with very flowery legalistic language and ask you to host some money (a very large amount of it) whilst the true owner escapes from some terrible situation. And you'll be paid handsomely for your help.
This scam appeals to your sense of humanity to help another, or to your sense of greed to help yourself.

There's only one action for these emails — Press delete.

There are too many types to list here, but you might find the links given in the appendix worth looking at next time you receive a hoax, or a phishing attempt.

Appendix 1 — Checklist for a great email

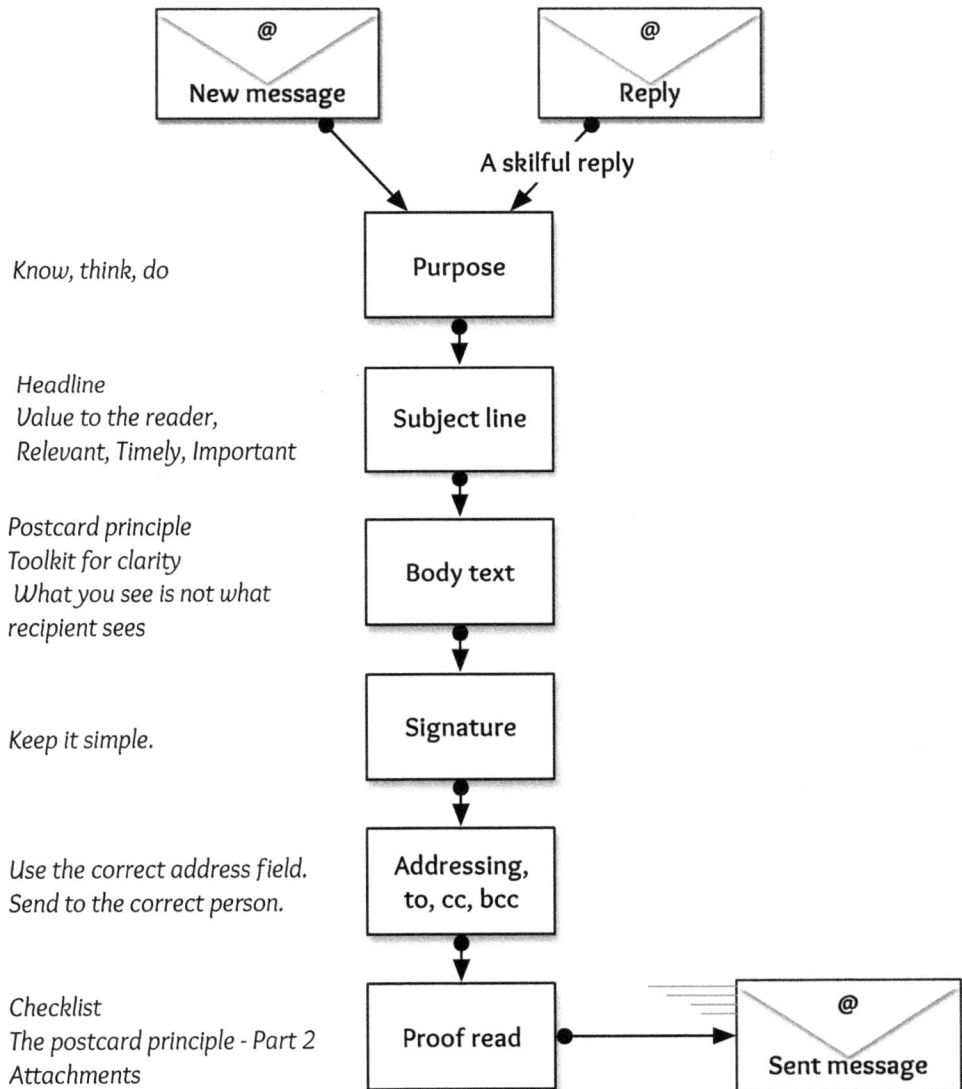

```
┌─────────────────────┐              ┌─────────────────────┐
│          @          │              │          @          │
│     New message     │              │       Reply         │
└─────────────────────┘              └─────────────────────┘
                                           A skilful reply
```

Know, think, do

```
                    ┌──────────────────┐
                    │     Purpose      │
                    └──────────────────┘
```

Headline
Value to the reader,
Relevant, Timely, Important

```
                    ┌──────────────────┐
                    │   Subject line   │
                    └──────────────────┘
```

Postcard principle
Toolkit for clarity
What you see is not what
recipient sees

```
                    ┌──────────────────┐
                    │    Body text     │
                    └──────────────────┘
```

Keep it simple.

```
                    ┌──────────────────┐
                    │    Signature     │
                    └──────────────────┘
```

Use the correct address field.
Send to the correct person.

```
                    ┌──────────────────┐
                    │   Addressing,    │
                    │    to, cc, bcc   │
                    └──────────────────┘
```

Checklist
The postcard principle - Part 2
Attachments

```
                    ┌──────────────────┐      ┌─────────────────────┐
                    │    Proof read    │─────▶│          @          │
                    └──────────────────┘      │    Sent message     │
                                              └─────────────────────┘
```

Appendix 2 — Metadata

Metadata is data about other data. For example, a picture from your digital camera contains the image data. It also has data about the image data. This is the metadata. The example shown, you can see what the image is. The metadata reveals what kind of camera was used, the settings used, and the date the picture was taken. This example harmless, but you have revealed unnecessary details to the recipient. Unless you take steps to remove metadata, it is in almost every file you create, and it stays with the file when you attach it to an email and send it to someone else. Some metadata is more revealing, potentially embarrassing, and gives away secrets you'd rather keep secret. In February 2003, 10 Downing Street published a document concerning Iraq. Unfortunately for the Prime Minister, the document was published as a Microsoft Word (.doc) document. Word documents carry a great deal of metadata. The metadata includes, amongst other things, a revision log, who has edited the document, which printer was used and so on. An enthusiastic journalist discovered the metadata, published the story and a political storm followed. The BBC covered this story — see it at

`news.bbc.co.uk/1/hi/technology/3154479.stm`

A more technical version is located here:

`www.computerbytesman.com/privacy/blair.htm`

Some modern versions of word-processors have security options to remove personal information; find out how to set these options on your system.

Portable documents (.pdf) carry metadata. In Adobe Acrobat, press Command-D (Mac) or Control-D (Windows) and you'll discover an interesting pot of information. If you generate portable documents, take control of this metadata before you send it to others. Metadata can land you in trouble.

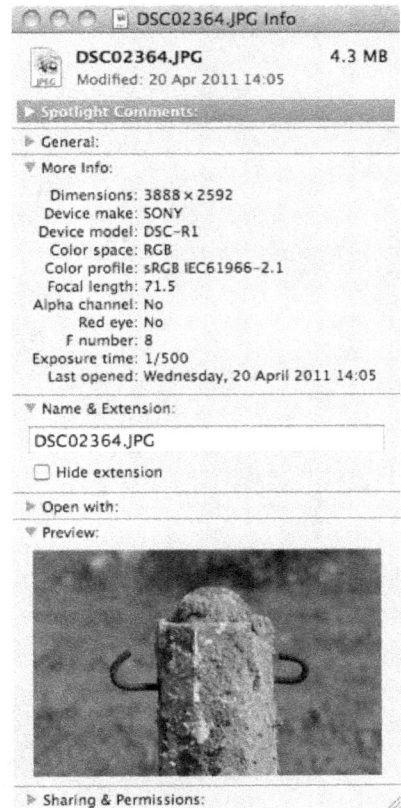

Appendix 3 — Emoticons, net speak, and jargon

This appendix is a catalogue of a few email emoticons, net-speak jargon, and management-jargon. Depending on the circumstances, an emoticon, or a few net-speak codes could be acceptable in your email. The standards and culture of your organisation should guide you here; in any case try not to compose an entire email of codes, your recipient's delete key is always at the ready.

These are a subset of those in common use. Some might be helpful where you and your recipient both know the shorthand code; some are definitely not for use in a business context. You must be the judge.

Emoticons

By the way (BTW) your word processor might have some of these in the Auto correct function. For example typing the smiley face code :-) is automatically replaced with ☺. The ☺ and ☹ are real characters in some fonts. A comprehensive listing. Is here:

en.wikipedia.org/wiki/List_of_emoticons

Emoticon	Meaning
:-)	Smiley face
;-)	Wink (light sarcasm)
:-|	Indifference
:->	Devilish grin (heavy sarcasm)
:-D	Shock or surprise
:-/	Perplexed
:-(	Frown (anger or displeasure)
:-P	Wry smile
:-Q	Smoker
:-e	Disappointment
:-@	Scream
:-O	Yell
:-*	Drunk
@}-;-'--,-	A rose
d(^_^)b	Wearing headphones

Net-speak

This subset, of the thousands in use, gives you a flavour of the vast range of net-speak codes. In a particular context, you might be able to work out what they mean by taking a second run at the sentence/paragraph. Perhaps you'll notice that many of these have an element of sarcasm. In an email it is easy to be brave at a distance; would you say the same thing to the person's face?

Net-speak code	Net speak de-coded
AAMOF	As A Matter Of Fact
AFAICS	As Far As I Can See
AFAIK	As Far As I Know
AFCPS	Any Fool Can Plainly See
ARE	Acronym-Rich Environment
ATB	All The Best
BCNU	Be seeing you
BFI	Brute Force and Ignorance. Bunch of Flipping Idiots
BKA	Better Known As
BOL	Best Of Luck
BTW	By the way
COB	Close Of Business
COTFL	Crawling On The Floor Laughing
EIF	Exercise In Futility
FWIW	For what it is worth
FYI	For your information
IIUC	If I Understand Correctly
IMBW	I May Be Wrong (Usually followed by 'But …')
IMHO	In my Humble Opinion
IMNSHO	In My Not So Humble Opinion
IMNSVHO	In My Not So Very Humble Opinion
IMO	In My Opinion
LOL	Laughing Out Loud. Lots Of Love/luck
LOLA	Laughing Out Loud Again
LOLOL	Lots Of Laughing Out Loud
LTR, L8R	Later
ROTFL	Rolling on the floor laughing
RTFM	Read the Fine/funny/flipping/*!*/ manual
TINSTAAFL	There's no such thing as a free lunch. TINSTA AFFL
TTFN	Ta Ta For Now
TTYL	Talk to you later

Just for fun — create a sentence using a minimum of words and a maximum net-speak. Beware of net-speak when the code has multiple meanings, for example:

You send — *Sorry I can't make it today; I'm going to a funeral. LOL*

>What you meant was LOL *(lots of love)*
>but the recipient read LOL *(laughing out loud).*

Remember your recipient makes the choice of how to interpret the net-speak, not you.

Consultant/Management speak

Management-speak phrases that sound inspirational or portray the speaker as an action oriented strategist (whatever one of those is!) However, most are meaningless fluff phrases. They don't really deserve a place in reports, especially not in an email where writing space and word count is at a premium. If you find yourself writing these, it is time for our best friend to take action. Head over to the delete key!

Accelerated technology/ learning/ deployment	Mission critical
At the end of the day	Move up the value chain
Best of Breed	Next Generation
Big ask	Paradigm shift
Downsizing/re-sizing/rightsizing/ de-layering	Push the envelope
Drop the ball	Put a stake in the ground
Firing on all cylinders/Cooking on gas	Run it up the flagpole and see who salutes
Game changing	Sustainability
Giving 110%	Synergy
Has legs and can go really far	Take it to the Next Level
Headcount	The Elephant in the room/corner
Heads up	Thinking outside of the box
it is not rocket science	Touch base
Let's hit the ground running	Uplift the goal
Low-hanging fruit	Where the rubber meets the road
Maximise customer satisfaction/ shareholder return	Win-win situation
Maximise leverage	You can't measure it, you can't control it.
	We're getting some push-back

Appendix 4 — The real cost of doing email

This guide has mentioned the impact of unnecessary emails. This impact has been expressed in terms of time. We covered two sources of where the time goes when doing emails:

1. The time it takes to process incoming emails

   - Those that come to you without your invitation.

   - Those you ask for, the 'copy me in' messages.

2. The lost-productivity time of regaining your train of thought following email interruptions

Converting time to money

As the old saying goes, time is money. So, convert time to money:

Convert your salary to cost of employment

Your salary is only one component of how much it costs to employ you. The other costs include, pension contributions, national insurance, and internal overheads (the cost of your paycheque, desk and phone, and support functions).

A rule of thumb is to multiply the salary by about 1.4 to give a Total Cost of Employment figure. The value 1.4 is an approximation for first-line supervisors, it rises to 1.8 for managers with employment benefits such as a company car. For very senior managers it can be 4 or more, especially if their remuneration has many aspects (healthcare, shares, and bonuses) — it depends on many factors.

If your salary is £25k × 1.4, your cost of employment as £35k

Convert your gross hours to nett hours.

You're not available to work for the whole time. There are 260 working days per year. From this, subtract the days for vacation, training, and illness.
This leaves about 210 nett days for doing work. Therefore ...

Your day rate is £35k ÷ 210 = £167 per day. For a 7½-hour day, it is about £22 per hour.

This gives us:

- The estimate of 21 hours per month *responding* to emails is £469. Equates to £5630 per year.

- The cost of *interruptions* is £17 per day equates to £3570 per year.

- The cost of *copy me in* emails is £95 per day equates to approximately £20k per year. Copy me in is a very expensive and unsustainable habit!

Desk exercise

The £22 above is an underestimate, because we haven't factored in the unproductive time during the day; chatting, making coffee, and so on. If the nett productive time is 75%, the £22 becomes approximately £31.50 per effective hour.

Calculate the examples with the higher figure.

Appendix 5 — Resources

19.5   Identifying fake emails

Suppliers of anti-virus software often have on-line resources to help you identify rogue emails. For example:

`www.snopes.com/computer/virus/virus.asp` or

`www.sophos.com/en-us/threat-center/threat-analyses/hoaxes.aspx`

Many banks have online security information on their web sites.

19.6   Bespoke resources

Do you have a need for bespoke resources?

For example:

- Customised versions of this book incorporating your own company's procedures and branding.

- Staff development through seminars or training.

- Facilitating project team kick-off workshops.

Please make contact via an email to `editor@leadership-library.co.uk`.

Appendix 6 — About the author

Alan Sarsby has enjoyed over forty years in varied careers, initially in electronic engineering, and IT strategy. Followed by customer service and business change. He has developed and implemented novel approaches to enterprise design and change leadership. In 2001, he established is own company specialising in training services. He is a conference speaker and non-fiction author.

Alan has many years' experience as a leadership trainer in blue-chip organisations. He is an expert in project leadership including the many associated tools, including the ability to influence and update stakeholders through effective presentation techniques.

Alan might be able to help you with:

- Training, workshops and seminars, conference speaking.

- Consulting services.

- Customised versions of this of this book to incorporate your own organisation's policies.

Contact: email to `editor@leadership-library.co.uk`

A dedicated web page for this book is here: `email.leadershipLibrary.uk` including updates and blog articles.

Your feedback

If this book has helped you we'd be delighted if you'd let us know. Alternatively, consider posting a review on the site where you obtained this book.

If you have suggested improvements, it would be good to know those too. And if you have ideas for similar subject matter, please send an email. Thanks.

All the best,

Alan.

ISBN 978-0-9932504-4-6

9 780993 250446